LOCATION, BORDERS AND BEYOND

THINKING WITH POSTCOLONIAL ART

IAIN MICHAEL CHAMBERS

WORLDING THE WORD

CONTENTS

Introduction	v
The stones in language	1
Whose modernity, whose home? The Western Desert art of Kathleen Petyarre	13
Troubled ground: disturbed foundations, translated cities	31
Unrealised democracy and art after humanism	45
Adrift and exposed: the art of Isaac Julien	59
Pushing History out of joint: art as anachronism	71
Acknowledgments	85
About the Author	87

Copyright © 2018 Iain Chambers
All rights reserved.

No part of this book may be reproduced in any form or by any electronic or mechanical means including information storage and retrieval systems, without permission in writing from the author. The only exception is by a reviewer, who may quote short excerpts in a review.

INTRODUCTION

What weaves through much of the following writing is the critical idea of art that leaves the shores of representation – the mimesis of some 'thing' that 'authentically' grounds the work – to propose an ethical event. Before the image I am asked to face, and face up to, the languages, histories and cultures that frame and inform the encounter. Sustained in a particular time in which past, present and future are rendered coeval and contemporary, the teleology of the art discourse, its history and aesthetics, is suspended: it is both exposed and called to account.

The very specificity of the image – the desert paintings of Kathleen Petyarre, the installations of Isaac Julien – that seemingly relays a discourse of identity and belonging, of being 'aboriginal' or 'black', betrays a secret history of art. For the work itself is not merely an addition to the existing canon – 'aboriginal culture', 'black art' – but becomes a critical interrogation and potential interruption that reconfigures its terms, reworks its tempos and reroutes its premises.

This is to transfer the work of art from the stilled status of an object to the active, subjecting force of a critical disposition. It invites us to think less of art and rather more with art; less to absorb passively the history of art and rather to work with art as a history that harbours a critical language still to be registered.

IMC

THE STONES IN LANGUAGE

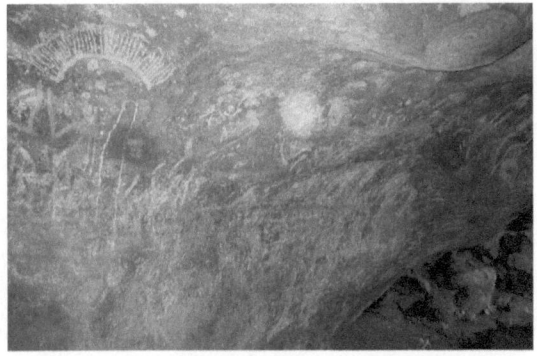

Uluru 2000

Conceived theatrically, outward movement neutralises the ground; it refuses to grant authority to anything except its own representations. In this way, local topographies become picturesque backdrops, easily dominated. At the same time, the actors of their own epic rarely do not see it like this. No sooner are they out of sight of land than all

> their talk is of homecoming, and the further they depart from the centre, the more they mutter of return. This is the magnetic power of the agora: to reverse the centrifugal charge, transforming it into centripetal nostalgia. Movement is deferred stasis, and who can blame lonely soldiers for massacring natives when they stand in their path, holding them up on their way home? What is more irritating to an actor that an unforeseen obstacle or distraction? It is axiomatic in the theatre that everything be arranged to facilitate the action. No wonder, then, that the indigenes are in the way.
>
> PAUL CARTER, THE LIE OF THE LAND, FABER & FABER, LONDON 1996, P.308

I HAVE JOURNEYED in the critical richness and complex dispersion of Paul Carter's writings, several times retracing my steps, in order to draw both sustenance and sense from an undertaking that, in insisting on the spatialisation of history, has radically reworked the very meaning of the modern historiographical operation. In the laying out or unfurling of time and being, in Carter's work the tranquillity of the library and seminar is transformed into an altogether more experimental, experiential, uneven and thorny environment. Some things persist in remaining opaque, untranslated: both beside, and beyond, the point I may be seeking to establish. Of course, it would be eminently correct to chart this development in concurrence with other voices that resonate in Carter's own trajectory. The names – Martin Heidegger, Michel Foucault, Michel de Certeau,

Jacques Derrida, Hayden White, Gilles Deleuze, but also Giambattista Vico, Paul Valéry, Paul Celan, T.G.H. Strehlow – fall on to the page. Still, that manner of academic registration is perhaps less important than navigating another atlas exposed in Carter's work, one that continually verges on the unmappable or indecipherable: that 'other half of a dialogue gone missing, as if the world had suddenly grown deaf, or the look been averted' (Paul Carter and Ruark Lewis, *Depth of Translation. The Book of Raft*, NMA Publications, 1999, p.69).

To insist on spatial history, both in terms of a particular intellectual archive and as an informative practice, is to push our language beyond the boundaries of an institutional and epistemological reckoning. It is to learn, not merely to read, but to listen to the dried-up river bed of the Finke River in the Northern Territory of Australia as a textured landscape that persistently 'speaks', even if we are unable to hear or understand its 'sounds'. If spatial history seeks to reference what simultaneously unfolds both towards us and away from us, it calls us with a voice that we can register and yet has a provenance elsewhere. In its wake we are invested by an ontological interrogation.

At a personal level, this particular journey could actually begin not far from the Finke River, in Alice Springs, among galleries full of Aboriginal art, backpacker hotels, and a rereading of Bruce Chatwin's literal evocation of indigenous 'songlines' in the town's public library. Crossing the bridge over the dried-up Todd River, a slightly inebriated Aboriginal informs us – two wide-eyed tourists, themselves slightly drunk on endless sky and space – that 'We Aboriginals are not bad people'. Beneath the bridge, huddled in the shade are makeshift shelters. Down the road in the West McDonnell Range is Hermannsburg, once home to Carl Strehlow, father of T.G.H. Strehlow, author of *Songs of Central Australia* and *Journey to Horseshoe Bend*. The latter being the chronicle of the last, desperate journey of his dying father, pastor of the Lutheran mission at Hermannsburg, down the Finke River to his death in a bush hotel at Horseshoe Bend.

Aboriginal peoples, missionaries, ranchers, anthropologists, linguists, historians, artists: this seemingly barren landscape, a desert in which the rivers are almost permanently dry, presents us, like a Clifford Possum Tjapaltjarri or Kathleen Petyarre painting, with a stratified and highly complex canvas, crisscrossed by diverse trajectories, interests and powers, subject to all the ambiguities, and possibilities, attendant on translation. Despite its obvious, blunt materiality, it is a territory that migrates. The sandy river bed, the bleached gum trees, the naked, red bluffs of the McDonnells, the 'lie of the land' under the noonday sun, is relayed in multiple languages that invest and renew the ground repeatedly. Suspended in a worldly network, the dense immediacy of locality and the powerful resonance of a planetary grammar are compounded in an uneven, even unstable, certainly inconclusive, mix. What is produced by this particular space is a critical locality that puts language and thought into movement, sets them in train, propels them on a journey that is 'improper' regarding any fixed sense of abode, authority and meaning.

In this migrant, travelling narrative, the geographical and historical possession of place (invariably the result of the dispossession of its previous occupants), its mapping of administrative, cultural and theoretical power, is itself dispossessed of finality and forced to account for itself on charts not always of its own making. Here place provides not an idle excuse for theoretical departures and homecomings, but rather, in researching and receiving its overlapping narratives and shifting grounds, the glimpse of a delicate geo-graphy: hesitant, incomplete, destined for decay and subsequent reworking. In this palimpsest of language, lives and time, the land, its rugged materiality, insists. Its insistence, however is not that of a perpetual truth but rather one of a temporal frame whose confines and borders set limits that simultaneously nurture the potential of transit.

Here the very idea of 'space', historically very much an Occidental abstraction and category, declines into contingent localities and circumstantial configurations. For language to live it must travel; it must enunciate its passage: in transit it augurs a 'translation without end' (Paul Carter and Ruark Lewis, *Depth of Translation. The Book of Raft*, NMA Publications, 1999, p.63). A stilled geometry is overwritten by a poetics that challenges the 'planar emptiness of historical space'. It is a poetics, a critical investment of language, that takes responsibility for the irreducible, where, in Paul Celan's phrase, language 'can be felt as a breath' (Paul Carter, *The Lie of the Land*, Faber & Faber, London 1996, p.294).

Carter's work presents us less with a stable archaeology, ready to be mined for lost historical forces and unsuspected sediments, than with an undulating series of landscapes in which history is always now. The 'lie of the land', to again cite the title of one of his works, evokes the uncertainty of the terrain across which the eye travels and from where the body receives its senses. The terrain is not merely an object or context to be appropriated, but is rather the limited, historical form, in which time and becoming occur. Carter's detailed excursion into its folds taps the inconclusive baroque logic that overflows in multiple directions to reveal the creased, underside of language, time, and a 'storied land'

(T.G.H. Strewlow, *Journey to Horseshoe Bend*, Rigby, Adelaide, 1978, p.218).

In the fold lies the depth, the profundity that never abandons the surface, the sensuous plane that grounds it all. Further, what is folded into time also unfolds across time: the plane of the senses also provides the potential for a temporary explanation (Gilles Deleuze, *The Fold*, Continuum, London, 2006). This is to tread the earth, 'that discontinuous, or folded, surface to which our ways of footing it is adapted', rather than to cross it mechanically with the result that one does 'not to know where to put one's feet' (Paul Carter, *The Lie of the Land*, Faber & Faber, London 1996, p.359, p.363). To exercise one's self on that ground is to take the measure of abstract, Occidental spatialisation. This, of course, stands in stark contrast to the 'classical' and universal sweep of those historians, geographers and cartographers of the human and social sciences who seek to return us to the sovereignty of the gaze that organises, explains and evaluates the panorama as, for example in Simon Scharma's *Landscape and Memory* (Fontana, London, 1996). The latter vision may be subtle, critically acute, but it remains ultimately untouched by the translation and the encounter with alterity that accompanies the recognition of a point of view being simultaneously assessed from elsewhere, located on a terrain where the (Occidental) subject can lose his or her bearings and unexpectedly be transformed into an object under other eyes.

In Amitav Ghosh's *In an Antique Land* the 'neutral' anthropologist becomes the flustered foreigner, unnerved by unsolicited questions disturbing his world when the 'objects' of his research – in Ghosh's case Egyptian peasants – research him and refuse to placidly lend authority to his discourse (Amitav Ghosh, *In an Antique Land*, Vintage,

New York, 1994). Local narratives run across and divert the abstract register of the authorial voice, interrogating the unilateral drive for self-confirmation, revealing maps and meanings that are perhaps undecipherable, that refuse to give up their secrets through insisting on their right to opacity, but that nevertheless persist as an inquiring presence. To bring such elements on stage, into the theatre of power and its telling, is to disturb the historical text that is being performed to legitimate – rarely 'to understand or interpret' – the nation, civilisation, progress and humankind (Paul Carter, *The Road to Botany Bay. An Exploration of Landscape and History*, Alfred Knopf, New York, 1988, p.xvi). This inducts us into another sense of mapping, one in which physical bodies are reintroduced, which, like pre-Colombian stone maps, requires one to walk around them in order to grasp the territory represented: that is to adopt a mobile, multiple point of view, rather than a unique vision.

Off-stage noises suggest that we might listen to what such a theatrics occludes, and begin to recognise that what we habitually refer to as History is precisely that: not the ordered unfolding of the single, transparent time of 'progress', but a particular modality of narrating the world which inadvertently alerts us to what it obscures – other, subaltern, denied forces and narratives. The uniqueness of this mode of telling lies not only in its assumed mantle of universal progress, but also, and more immediately, in its desire to render its power legitimate by any means (military, political, economical, juridical, cultural) possible. Such power constantly steps out of bounds in moments of 'emergency' (which, as Walter Benjamin and Giorgio Agamben have taught us, threaten to become permanent) to reaffirm its authority. It suspends the 'law', and brutally exposes the violence of its own legal fictions, thereby establishing the boundaries that serve to separate its self-realisation from the rest of the world precisely in the instance that it takes possession of the world. This hegemony 'which reduces space to a stage, that pays attention to events unfolding in time alone, might be called imperial history' (*ibid*).

What spills out of this implacable linearity, what falls out of the frame, beyond the explanation, what is apparently without history 'are analogous to unfinished maps and should be read accordingly as records of travelling' (*ibid*., p.xxii). Here in the vicinity of Edward Said and James Clifford, the histories of travel and the travel of thought introduce us to the idea of moving in a different historical space, not simply a history within History, nor simply a movement within an existing language, but rather a fundamental re-articulation of that very language: 'Such spatial history... begins and ends in language' (*ibid*., p.xxiii). What history once silenced, interred and effaced is transformed into the baroque poetics of a *tombeau*: an exhumation and revisitation of language, a poetic configuration that releases the past into the present, flowing along the paths of a multilateral constellation, destined to frustrate 'the Western sense of an ending' (Paul Carter, *The Lie of the Land*, Faber & Faber, London 1996, p.292). As Carter himself puts it:

> To take account of the lie of the land is not simply to seek to ground historical knowing differently; it is to break down the opposition between history and poetry. What if, say, the manner of going over the ground were itself a poetic act, and not merely a prosaic means of getting from one place to another?

LOCATION, BORDERS AND BEYOND 9

PAUL CARTER, THE LIE OF THE
LAND, FABER & FABER, LONDON
1996, P.295.

Such a history is not exhausted by the naming, colonisation and appropriation of the other. It prospects a differentiated, negotiated envelopment by time and tempos that are neither simply unilateral nor necessarily mono-rhythmic. Here the teleology of the all-seeing gaze is blinded, bent and diverted in the performative poetics of place, where curvilinear horizons promoted by the earth disturb and dislocate the tabular rationale of the map. Tony Gatlif's marvellous film *Latcho Drom* (1993) on the migrating musicality of the Roma from Rajasthan to Spain, for example, installs a narrative sustained by the journey of sound. The music of being and the being of music distinguish a trail, a path that travels from horizon to horizon, disseminating song, dance and music that reworks an obvious and unquestioned understanding of belonging and the presumed coda of homecoming. The music sustains the passage of a poetics that unfolds beneath the sky of a world which does not necessarily originate from our actions. In this instance of panic, that uncanny premonition of uncertainty, doubt and homelessness, we recognise, even if we immediately go on to deny it, that we are held in languages that are not necessarily of our own making; languages that arrive from elsewhere and unfold towards who knows where. This, as Paul Carter justly reminds us, is 'the poetics of the storm' that announces the baroque (*Ibid.*, 299). It is precisely here that the 'tactics of colonisation (temporarily at least) fail, where for a while irremediable differences communicate without ceding ground (*Ibid*).

In such a critical disposition, replete with 'baroque memories', the language of mimesis gives way to an altogether more ragged narrative that arrives through a rent in Occidental sense to insist on another way of telling, another way of being, in which the gesture of the body, the performance of a poetics, the distillation of becoming in a sound, exceeds the conclusive logic of a monument, a book, a map, an archive, a law (Paul Carter, *Baroque Memories*, Carcanet, Manchester, 1994). What returns us to a ground, snatches from beneath our feet the flat carpet of abstract pretensions, temporarily frees us from the deadly teleology of the infinite 'progress' of accumulation and releases us into another world. It is this re-inscription of our selves within the contours of 'the continuing critique of Western Logos that will characterise the emergence of a post-colonial polity and poetry' (Paul Carter, *The Lie of the Land*, Faber & Faber, London 1996, p.302.

All of this complicates the unilateralism of the gaze as it comes to be seeded with the auditory dimension that leaves space for a reply. It sets an inherited way of seeing into movement, deprives it of a privileged viewpoint, renders its linearity vulnerable to other gazes that cross, deviate and interrupt its path. The world brought under different eyes, without the guarantees provided by a fixed perspective, allows us to consider that what we look upon we often do not see, for 'even visually, the world is folded, containing the unseen within the seen...' (*Ibid.*, p.304). The linguistic tyranny that organises our perception – the implacable linearity of subject and predicate, noun and verb – negates the multilateral coexistence of the manifold voices that stab the silence, that echo and envelope a differentiated, terrestrial communality. To reintroduce this undisciplined disturbance is to challenge the language that 'refuses to grant authority to anything except its own representations'; it is to insist on the 'environmental charge' that ignites the space of history (*Ibid.*, p.309, p.311). The acts that occur there can neither be prescribed nor rehearsed. Their ambiguity can be reduced, put into a tale, narrated with ends in mind, but never exhaustively 'explained' nor conclusively defined. There remains, as both challenge and comfort, the insistence of the world that pushes through the masque in a historical inscription that grounds us in the persistent poetics of always becoming.

WHOSE MODERNITY, WHOSE HOME? THE WESTERN DESERT ART OF KATHLEEN PETYARRE

Kathleen Petyarre, Mountain Devil Lizard 2005 (80x 79 synthetic polymer paint on Belgian linen)

TO CONSIDER the articulation of identities, caught between the insistence of power and the fragmentary prose and potential of the world, is, most obviously, to consider the performative instance, the 'now', in which historical conditions and their accompanying cultural, political and economic possibilities are brought together in temporal configurations on the body, through the tongue, across the psyche This, as a minimum, suggests that there are no such things as fixed or everlasting identities. Perhaps we need to ponder on such processes as they spiral back and burrow through the assumed stability of our understandings of the self. Our point of departure, our 'selves' become suspect; the subject an object for another discourse, for an 'other'. It is here, of course, and most obviously, that the one-time 'objects' of aesthetic, anthropological, social and cultural attention respond as historical subjects, subjecting us to their interrogative presence.

This opens up the vista, for some unnerving, of the previously subaltern, marginal and peripheral interrogating and reconfiguring the languages, technologies and techniques of the hegemonic and the assumed primacy of its languages and understandings. What is probably most disquieting, uncanny in the deepest reach of that expression, is witnessing how such languages and associated powers, come to be re-located, re-written and re-articulated, so that they come to speak of other worlds within the tissues and textures of our own. They speak through us, through me, as it were, of other ways of being in time and place. In Berlin a hundred other Berlins now open up. The seeming opposites of 'our' modernity (although a sense of ownership is here clearly slipping beyond our grasp) – the cosmopolitan and the 'primitive', the 'archaic' and the avant-garde – are rendered immediate and proximate. Their being con-temporary within modernity provokes poles of mutual interrogation.

This is a modernity that might include that fifty per cent of the world's population that has never made a phone call in its life, just as it might also include an invitation to consider London a Muslim city and New York a displaced Caribbean one. Here I would have to consider modernity in the 'outraged light' (Adrienne Rich) of those whose labour and subjugation have been central to its making, although they have systematically remained peripheral to its official accounting of time, to its History. This would be to consider 'progress' from the shadows, in terms of the hunger, humiliation, ultimately slavery and genocide, that has stalked its uncoiling across the globe over the last five centuries.

To hear this tale I would also have to reconsider the

project of the seeming simple, but impossible, task of harnessing the non-western world to a linear and homogeneous sense of development and 'progress'. At this point it might rather be the case to punctuate and interrupt that narrative and associated powers with a more complex, untidy, heterogeneous and altogether more critical configuration. This is where the 'civilising' trip up the Congo turns out to be a journey into the growing darkness of the world where I am ultimately brought face to face with the horror: the horror that resides in the heartlands of Occidental modernity, in the very making and realisation of my 'self'.

If my own identity is in debt to this heritage, to an underlying racist, colonial and imperial formation, invariably wrapped up in the neatly ascetic and whitewashed hues of modernity, then considerations of constructions of the self – both the self that is affirmed and the self that is negated – opens on to an altogether wider and more disturbing horizon of questions. The power to speak and represent a self, to seemingly construct an identity within the available languages of the world, is neither simply given nor automatically guaranteed. Not everyone is able to consider the question. While some have the means to choose with what and how to identify, others – the natives, the aboriginals, the masses, the working classes (and the nineteenth slide from the jungles of Africa to those of the modern metropolis was certainly deliberate), black people, Muslims – seemingly have an identity thrust upon them.

What becomes significant in such a situation is the development and distribution of sense – not merely the seeming stability of a semantic order but, above all, the impulse of transit and the inauguration of a direction (*sens*) – between these seemingly stark and incommensurable alternatives. Here, along the border, in the frontier between the subject and the subjected, there emerge a series of mediations, of transits, translations and transformations, that bequeath an important political and ontological fallout on both sides of an apparently permanent divide. Perhaps I can only come to my senses in the presence of the other, alongside an other. It comes as no surprise that it is in the unruly unfolding of language along such fractures and frontiers, and in its custody for the unexpected, the disquieting and the extraordinary, in other words as poetics and art, that we can most readily register a construction of the self that is neither taken-for-granted nor merely resisted or rejected.

I wish to sustain this argument by proposing a brief journey that starts from nowhere. Nowhere is also Utopia, from the Greek *ou-topos*: non-place. Actually Utopia exists on maps. The one that I am referring to is located some 250 kilometres northeast of Alice Springs in Australia's Northern Territory.

It came to my attention through the prolific production of the artists, many of whom are Aboriginal women, whose works are on display in the galleries in Alice. These remarkable dot paintings, often measuring several metres in height and width, allow me to consider how the non-metropolitan world is revealed to be also a part of our world in the unexpected fusion of the so-called 'archaic' and the artistic avant-garde. This is neither to evoke the erotics of distance, nor a fetishism of the exotic, but is rather to consider the immediacy of what, in the circuits of international art and aesthetics, lies proximate but ultimately irreducible to my domestication. Here the banality of the tourist gaze can be drawn into a deeper and more extensive cultural economy, and there encounter more radical reconsiderations and reconfigurations of modernity.

Between the aboriginal and the avant-garde, between

the ethnographic museum and the modern art gallery, between the archaic and the absolutely modern, emerges both the confusion and the cross-fertilisation of aesthetic and cultural discourse in the languages of being a contemporary Aboriginal. I have chosen these paintings precisely because they occupy such an ambiguous ground. Seemingly 'authentic' in their rural, desert 'origins' and their sacred subject matter of ancestral dreamings, their unsolicited proximity to Western and avant-garde art – due to their inevitable enmeshing in the exotic and archaic labels they are destined to carry – produces an uncanny ground that stretches beyond the altogether more explicit political protest of much contemporary, particularly urban, Aboriginal art.

In these canvases there emerge a series of questions that carry us beyond the conscious opposition of individuals into an altogether more extensive, post-humanist polity. Drawn into this more insidious 'politics', one that is not immediately dependent on the individual volition of the modern, self-conscious subject, this space proposes 'interactions between cultures that may remain on radically different ground' (Nicholas Thomas, *Possession:Indigineous Art/Colonial Culture*, Thames & Hudson, London, 1999, p.17). As Rosi Braidotti has put it: 'Politics in this framework has as much to do with the constitution and organisation of affectivity, memory and desire as with consciousness and resistance' (Rosi Braidotti, 'The Paradox of Nomadic Embodied Subjectivity', *Textus*, XIII, 2, 2000).

Alongside the obvious and complex contract with the colonising aggressor, these canvases, destined for non-Aboriginal viewers, reveal a negotiated assimilation of the international art market which, in turn, provides the means for living on, survival, in terms not wholly dictated by the culture and society that such a market represents. These works emerge not only from a precise location, whose cultural complexity and symbolic depth is difficult for me to imagine, but also from a diverse temporality, in which the linear pragmatics of 'progress' and the unfolding history of modernist art is displaced, if not absent. Yet these works, even if not fully susceptible to a modernist index, are also very much a part of the modern world. They, too, are contemporary.

In this manner, Western Desert art is not about an absolute alterity, or merely the archaic seeding the avant-garde; it represents rather a 'kind of colonial negotiation': a localised becoming sited in the Northern Territory, rather than an abstract Aboriginality (Paul Carter, *The Lie of the Land*, Faber & Faber, London, 1996, p.348). This is signalled in the very materiality of the representation. Acrylic paint, canvas and the drive towards aesthetic permanence, were all brought into the Aboriginal communities of the Western Desert in the 1970s by white educators, initially at Papunya. True, there already existed the seeming endurance of rock paintings and engravings, but even these, like the altogether more momentary expression of sand drawings, body and bark paintings, along with decorated artefacts, were intrinsic to the transit of nomadic life.

Western Desert art, as a complex response to the changed conditions of being 'Aboriginal', represents a radical twist in that tale. Beyond the stark divide between the colonised and the coloniser, and the generalised assumption of the 'fatal impact' on the former's culture, there emerges from precise localities and historical conditions something whose complexity is patently modern. At the same time, within the hybrid endorsement of transnational cultural reception in public galleries and private homes, these works continue to adhere to another place; they remain other-wise. While it is not that particular story that I will be pursuing here, I will be speaking in its disquieting vicinity by dialoguing in an oblique manner with the work of the Aboriginal artist Kathleen Petyarre.

Land, language and locality are clearly on display here, overwhelmingly indexed in the ubiquity of the artist's Dreaming Ancestor – Old Woman Mountain Devil or Thorny Devil Lizard – announced in the titles of nearly all of her works. If I cannot speak of the sacred symbology of ancestral dreaming tracks and 'song lines', that is not my 'business', I can still seek to respond to their provocative proximity in terms of how I might return to the question of art, aesthetics, and my sense of being in a world in which these paintings are also a part (also the conclusion I would draw from Bruce Chatwin's literary 'walkabout' in *The Songlines*). This, to echo Nicholas Thomas's words, is 'to raise a wider question about the space and time of contemporary art' (Nicholas Thomas, *Possession:Indigineous Art/Colonial Culture*, Thames & Hudson, London, 1999, p.217).

The work, in more senses than one, is framed. The frame, as a border, a limit, finitude, horizon, draws attention to what simultaneously unfolds into the artwork and what unfolds away and out of the picture. Along this border the generic marker between the work and the world is extended to accommodate uncertainties and an indecision concerning the conclusion of one and the appearance of the other. The frame, as a liminal zone that evokes the interval between the poetical and the pedestrian, is ultimately osmotic, permeable. It installs a membrane that filters bilateral traffic: the world as exteriority is present, just as the particular work resonates with its place in the world. So the frame is also a limit, not so much in the sense of setting the poetic off from the everyday, but rather in inscribing a location – historical, cultural, political, gendered... thus temporal, hence mortal – in the very configuration of the work.

To approach the work's enframing in this manner is to acknowledge a simultaneous closure and aperture: the conjoining of the specificity of the art work, its style, tradition and execution, with the context or ontological ground on which it depends and out of which it develops. It is here that the poetical and the prosaic, hence the aesthetical and the ethical, acquire an alarming intimacy.

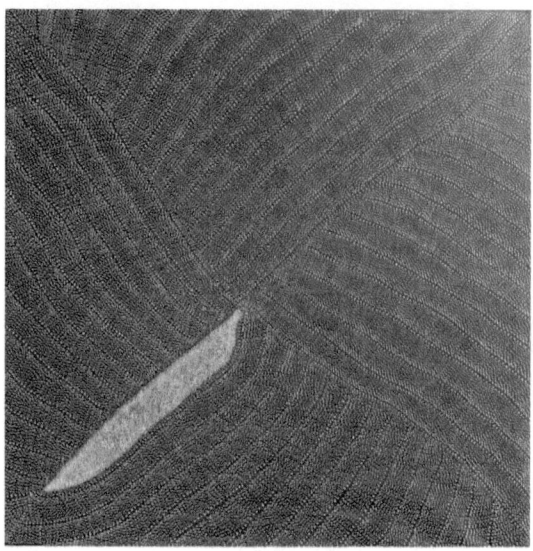

Kathleen Petyarre, Mountain Devil Lizard Dreaming, 2007 (120 x 120, synthetic polymer paint on Belgian linen)

Let's consider the 'flatness' of these paintings. They proffer emotional maps and local narratives that refuse perspective, hence no privileged place for the viewing subject. This refusal of perspective disturbs the classical subject-object relationship that confirms the former by putting her or him in the picture (both physically: the view that unfolds outwards from the European eye/I towards the horizon; and metaphysically: the perspective that confirms the subject as origin of the gaze). Of course, this argument can be made with all modern, non-representational art from Russian constructionism to Rothko.

The absence of depth, previously afforded by perspective, leads to the dispersal of the subjective point of view. For what we are looking at here is precisely compounded and complicated by an expression whose language is performed across that violent historical displacement of colonialism and empire that haunts the subject-centred humanism of the West. The return of the repressed flattens things out, creates a new situation, dare one say a temporary democracy before the canvas, in a shared, de-centred space. This suggests that such works persistently propose something lying beyond the hyphen of postcolonial hybridity (itself often an unconscious extension of the universality of Occidental humanism). For here something sticks out, endures in its claims to history and place, in the very currents of modernity. We, too, are invited to consider such disquieting claims, and the accompanying impossibility of synthesis, as part of our history. 'A hyphen is never enough to conceal protests, cries of anger or suffering, the noise of weapons, airplanes, and bombs' (Jacques Derrida, *Monolingualism of the Other; or, The Prosthesis of Origin*, Stanford University Press, Stanford, 1998, p.11).

If these works are also part of our world, of our modernity, and they most clearly are, what does that imply? Are we merely dealing in aesthetic objects, and the accompanying sensations that serve to enliven our routines, enrich our sensibilities? Are we simply the cultural guardians of this accumulation, as it is we who buy and judge the works that enter the category of art? It is there that we possess them; or do these works bring something more in their train?

Of course, for many in the museums, art galleries, specialist magazines and collector's living rooms, a universalist sense of aesthetics (invariably underwritten by global market value) is more than sufficient justification for the principle of accumulation that continues to confirm the humanist subject who remains at the centre of the picture: cataloguing, categorising and evaluating the world that mirrors his or her point of view. To acknowledge that there is something else that breaks the circuits of cultural and economical capital would be to accommodate consideration of the unruly supplement these works propose. The fact that they are not merely aesthetical or modern in any singular sense invites us to reconsider the humanist paradigm and premises that apparently controls and disciplines the passage of such canvases and artefacts through the world. We are clearly dealing with something altogether more significant than the mere revaluation or extension of the earlier marginalising categories of 'primitive', 'ethnic', 'native' or 'minority' art.

This perhaps implies taking the liberal humanist lexicon seriously by bringing it to account for its responsibilities in overseeing and framing the world. So, the centrality of the construction of the self and its freedom become pressingly pertinent, although altogether more disturbingly concrete, in the historical and cultural claims of subaltern and indigenous identifications. This is to suggest less a series of negotiated entries and exits from modernity by minority groups and forces, and rather the duplication and dispersal of modernity from different positions, locales and languages within modernity itself. This would be to shift modernity away from its assumed roots in a precise geopolitical terrain in the West, and its accompanying claims of ownership and management, and propose its reconfiguration in a shifting, worldly constellation, cleaving an uncharted path through the contingent impurities of historical time.

Considered in this manner, the seemingly exotic choice of Western Desert dot paintings, drawn apparently from one of the furthest points of the earth, is, beyond the obvious enclosure of the tourist gaze, dramatically proximate to the critical languages and projects many of us are involved in. Speaking in the vicinity of these works I am able to acknowledge what I can and might desire to say, while simultaneously also forced to acknowledge what I cannot articulate. Moving beyond the limits of an inherited European representation is to enter the space of non-sense, ultimately the potential death of my meaning. Herein lie the trauma, violence and horror of so much of the modern colonial experience. Where there is no reflection of my self, where, despite my objectifying, cataloguing and calculating, things refuse my reason, then remove, negate, even exterminate.

Today, it may be necessary for us, for me, to die a little to live further. To register from within my own historical and cultural lexicon what cannot be revealed, what remains unknown and unknowable (and refuses obvious accommodation in the consolidated categories of the sublime and the sacred) is to confront what exceeds my immediate life, language and understanding.

To acknowledge this state is to sabotage the infinite and lethal pretensions of the occidental humanist paradigm.

This, however, is not to resign oneself to mere cultural relativism; it is, rather, to announce the universal complexities of a shared historical constellation whose light, shape, powers and consequences vary from locale to locale. Events have occurred, lives have been lived, and bodies and voices, even in the stunning interrogation of silence, live on, shadow and interrogate my own accounting of time. As Walter Benjamin argued, and as Pier Paolo Pasolini most beautifully explored in his cinema, the past comes to meet us from the future.

In such a light these paintings propose the language of the stranger who announces the memory of the dead: the testimony of the forgotten who recall the threshold of another way of being in the world. This space is therefore also the space of death for European representation and its hegemony of realism. Rendering the world transparent to its will, hence susceptible to a unilateral and universal gaze, is no doubt what explains the overwhelming allegiance of Occidental modernity to the murderous power of realism: it figuratively and literally kills others and reduces them to objects in order to secure its point of view. What cannot be represented, rendered acceptable to the subject's reason, is eliminated: an apparent naturalness is secured by the violence exercised in the margins that guarantees its framing (Jon Stratton, 'The Banality of Representation: Generation, Holocaust, Signification and "Empire of Senseless"', *New Formations,* 51). For the paradox of realism is that its unilateral, subject-centred representation depends on the repression of other points of view. Here the undoing of realism proposes the undoing of occidental humanism as the universal measure of the world.

Held in a historical constellation where meaning emerges from limits, rather than from the timeless universality of abstract concepts, the art work here presents us with a horizon of language, worldly location and terrestrial framing, that lies behind us, before us, and beyond us. This is a sense of meaning that emerges from within the material constraints of a historical configuration that is, precisely for such reasons, both locatable and ultimately without permanent or timeless foundations. In time and of time, such meaning constitutes a 'way' (Heidegger), a 'passage' (Benjamin) that registers a position and a responsibility for location, for a voice, rather than the universal, accumulative, 'progress' that instrumental rationality seeks to amass around itself. It is in this sense, both historically and politically, beyond the scale and the pale of existing humanism.

The sense of art that I am seeking to evoke here amidst the interrogative presence of these paintings lies within proximity of an edge, announcing a threshold that recalls the opening that sustains us and sends us on our way. All of this is quite distinct from the simple shock and sensationalism that merely confirms the institutional grammar of the everyday and the mundane. It is a question of a serious unsettling, a rendering homeless, of a previous sense and the subsequent direction of thinking, being and becoming. This reveals us in an uncanny location, simultaneously recognising our limits while being solicited with the possibility of considering what exists beyond inherited confines. It should also be noted that such a displacement is also true for previously, settled indigenous authorities, such as that of Aboriginal Australia or Maori Aotearoa. It is the mutual consequences and interlacing of such unsettling historical processes, and their subsequent cultural configurations, that today establish the troubled ambiguity of a postcolonial horizon of sense.

To register such limits is to step away from a self-absorption which turns language, history, culture and the world over to a sterile, ultimately deadly, preoccupation with property: 'my' language', 'their' culture, 'our' history. To step away and propose art, language and history in a more dispossessed manner is to render proximate the uncomfortable promise of displacement and alterity. This is certainly not an art of sublimation, something that merely allows me to relax secure in the contemplation of self-confirmation. For it is to propose neither integration nor domestication, but rather a constellation that irritates and interrogates institutional and inherited understandings.

Simply to recognise in alterity the relativity of previous claims to absolute sense, knowledge and truth, does not necessarily dislocate the subject's continuing pretence to self-realisation through the objectification of the other; the continuity of that relationship, even relativised and historicised, can remain fundamentally untouched. It is rather when the observer takes in hand her or his illusions and self-centredness that it becomes possible for the subject finally 'not to speak of, but close by' (Assia Djebar, *Femmes d'Alger dans leur appartment*, 1980; reprised by Trinh T. Minh-ha in her film *Reassemblage*, 1982). Having largely dispossessed the other I have now to learn to dispossess myself of the power to dispossess.

It is here that the dominion of the Western art market – its institutions of criticism, galleries and museums – is inadvertently forced to overreach itself in housing works of art that reveal other worlds (in which the very idea of 'art', the 'artist' and the aesthetic as an autonomous quality may be absent, or else subsumed in another agenda).

In this attempted domestication, the very categories – ethnic, primitive, 'Third World', indigenous – that previously sought to catalogue (and contain) these works, rendering them subaltern to the disposition of the Euro-American art discourse, become increasingly brittle. Aboriginal artists like Kathleen Petyarre who continue to live, work and sustain themselves in the 'outback', as in diverse fashion, cosmopolitan postcolonial artists who inhabit the urban networks of the overdeveloped world, belong to more than one category. Not only does such art, seemingly from elsewhere but actually and profoundly proximate, often directly relay a relationship to the grounding of locality and the earth in its symbolic materiality (while not necessarily ignoring the Western, academic and avant-garde discourse into which it has also been inserted), but also its very being requires a response that breaches the confines of the hegemonic logic that is apparently explaining it. It represents what Jean François Lyotard defined as the differend: the undoing of a common measure, hence the solicitation of something else that seriously shakes the possibility of commensurability.

By resurrecting in our midst not merely a plurality of worlds this art, once labelled 'primitive', 'native', 'aboriginal' or 'ethnic', but now equally cosmopolitan in its marketing and sometimes, but not always or necessarily, in its execution, dramatically draws us into the interval between the earth and a world, between a terrestrial context and an immediate habitat. There it offers us a diverse configuration of that encounter. This 'other art' is not a wholesale alternative existing to represent a primordial 'authenticity' that challenges the presumed inauthenticity of modernity, but is rather an 'other' view that opens up a gap, an interval, between the accustomed and the unknown, between a world and another. It here permits the question of our becoming to continue to continue, for it is an art that simultaneously interrupts and interprets modernity. Despite their seeming unfamiliarity, such works are also intrinsic to our familiarity: their 'unfamiliar familiarity' betrays their profoundly uncanny character (Ken Gelder and Jane Jacobs, *Uncanny Australia. Sacredness and Identity in a Postcolonial Nation,* Melbourne University Press, Melbourne, 1998, pp.23-7).

In this opening, in this rift installed by the act of painting, by a film, a piece of music, prose or poetry, the perceived alterity of the art work and its particular 'origins' splices the assumed singularity of a planetary logic with the thread of the transnational which, as the site of multiple, and by no means unilateral, translation, is where idealised 'authenticities' are inevitably travestied. Here lies the debate on creolité, on hybridity, on métissage, that can also stumble into the dark heart of a cultural and historical refusal to hyphenate. The apparent homogeneity of the institutional discourse of art – still largely managed through the occidental abstractions of culture and the aesthetic – is now interrogated by the same work simultaneously occupying diverse modalities: as object of our humanist, academic gaze (aesthetic and commercial fetishism), as ritual, mythical or religious sign (ontic difference), as a cultural and historical way of being (ontological difference). This is all held together in the composite drift across the border between the religious aura and the secular art object, sustained in the rendezvous of the radical sublime that breaches its earlier conceptual borders to indicate an unsuspected custody for a counter-history of modernity. It is here that the separation of the sacred from the prosaic becomes impossible without destroying that surfeit of incommensurability and untranslatability that is the sublime itself.

The composite effect of such differences, irreducible to a single explanation or site, works to promote a multifarious 'dynamics of change' rather than the flat index of 'progress' (Gilane Tawadros in Jean Fisher (ed.) *Global Visions: Towards a New Internationalism in the Visual Arts*, Kala Press, London, 1994). It is where, to refer to the unabsorbed supplement these works expose, it is where situated, rather than synthetic, understandings are elaborated.

Experiencing and exploring the rift between the potential of terrestrial becoming and the immediate limits of the local world I inherit and inhabit, the artwork here becomes central. It no longer pertains either to distanced exotica, or to idealised aesthetics, but is proximate and interrogative. For it discloses the interval between the ordinances of the world and its interruption by what both exhumes and eschews the fragility of that order. That is why art, as opposed to the consolatory techniques of reproducing the familiar, is invariably shocking, even terrible. It refuses to be domesticated, it arrests our world, and in rendering it extraordinary sharply exposes its restrictive nature by enhancing the promise of our 'capacity to be' (Heidegger). With that, and hoping that this brief journey has added some further considerations, I will conclude.

TROUBLED GROUND: DISTURBED FOUNDATIONS, TRANSLATED CITIES

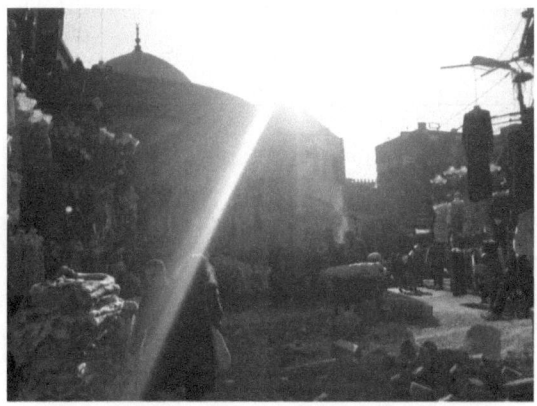

Cairo 2012

Progress itself is not something that unfolds in a single line. Along with the natural weakening an idea suffers as it becomes diffuse, there is also the criss-crossing of influences from new sources of ideas. The innermost core of the life of every age, an inchoate, swelling mass, is poured into moulds

> forged by much earlier times. Every present period is simultaneously now and yet millennia old. This millipede moves on political, economic, cultural, biological and countless other legs, each of which has a different tempo and rhythm. One can see this as a unified picture and elaborate it in terms of a single cause by always keeping to a central perspective...but one can also find satisfaction in the exact opposite. There is no plan in this, no reason: fine. Does this really make it any uglier than if there were a plan?
>
> ROBERT MUSIL, "NOTES FOR READERS WHO HAVE ELUDED THE DECLINE OF THE WEST", 1921

TO THINK of the modern city – Cairo, London, Istanbul, Lagos or Buenos Aires – is to experience a perpetual translating machine. Here economical, cultural and historical forces are configured and acquire local form, substance and sense. These days much attention is given to how global flows become local realities in the multiple realisations of processes of 'glocalisation', but the archive that the city proposes represents an altogether deeper sedimentation of time and place.

Cities as the sites of cultural encounters – from fifth century Athens with its Greeks, Persians and Egyptians, to present-day multi-cultured Los Angeles – are precisely where the outside world proposes immediate proximities. In this context, differences may also be accentuated: think of the ghettoes and ethnic areas and communities of many a modern Euro-American city. Cultural and historical overspills, most immediately registered in culinary, musical and cultural taste, do not automatically lead to physical conviviality and friendship. Nevertheless, even if we cling to familiar accents, the grammar of the city continually undergoes transformation. This occurs without our consent.

We inevitably find ourselves speaking in the vicinity of other histories and cultures, proximate to others who may refuse our terms of translation, insist on opacity and refuse to be represented in our reason. As a translating and translated space, the language of the city is never merely a linguistic matter. For what is being 'spoken' in a mixture of asymmetrical powers is precisely the intricate accumulation of historical encounters established in the conjunctural syntax of a particular urban cultural formation. As the concentrated site of such processes, and their augmented velocity, the city continually proposes the urgency of considering life, both ours and that of others, in the transit proposed by translation.

What precisely might this mean? Beyond the obvious threshold of translation inaugurated by the arrival of the other, the stranger, invariably required to transform his history and her culture into our language and understanding, there emerges the disquieting insistence that we, too, are somehow being translated by unacknowledged processes in the very city that we consider our own. This leads us onto troubled ground. The foundations of our history and culture, of our lives and sense of belonging, are disturbed. The assurance of a domestic place is exposed to unauthorised and unplanned questioning. Literally transported elsewhere, we are translated.

For what is rendered explicit in translation is not merely the contingency of language and our movement in its midst, but also the persistent interrogation seeded by ambiguity, uncertainty, reformulations, semantic shifts and contestation: the uncontrolled passage of language elsewhere, and the right to the irreducible opacity theorised by Édouard Glissant. The provocative and productive force of translation, as a continual negotiation of being in the world, can be traced in multiple forms and formations: in the phenomenology of everyday life, in musical, pictorial and literary aesthetics, in clothing and culinary practices, in debating questions of faith, in renewing the lexicon of philosophical and critical discourse... Among the many ways of thinking of such processes, processes that are intrinsic to the making of the modern city and the modernity it is presumed to represent, is that provoked by critical considerations of contemporary architecture and urban planning.

Architecture as the material and technical appropriation of ground, history and memory proposes a problematic site of power and politics, of technics, technology and aesthetics. All of this is unconsciously secreted in the seemingly neutral grid lines of the survey, the plan and the project. If architecture provides us with a habitat, a home, it also contributes to the language in which ideas of home, identity and domesticity, and the supposed opposites of the unhomely, the non-identical and the foreign, are conceived and received. This renders space both problematical and partisan: no longer an empty, 'neutral' container, waiting to be filled by the abstract protocols of 'progress', but rather the site of a complex and troubled inheritance that questions all desires to render it transparent to a conclusive logic. So, opening up the languages of building, administrative planning and architectural projection, seeding them with doubt, and crisscrossing their concerns with lives lived, living and yet to come, is to render the 'laws' of cultural codification vulnerable to what they seek to contain and control. Every act of representation is simultaneously an act of repression. Every excluded trace becomes the site of a potential transformation, the point of departure for unsuspected developments.

So, despite the presumption of the explorer's map and the architectural drawing board, space is never empty; it is has already been inhabited, nominated and produced by some body. Abstract coordinates are themselves the purified signals of altogether more turbulent and terrestrial transit. In this stark affirmation lies a profound challenge to an eye/I that has historically been accustomed to colonising a space considered 'empty' before its occupation by Occidental 'progress'. Against a grade zero of history inaugurated by the West, its languages, disciplines, technologies and political economy, it is ethically and aesthetically possible to pose the historical heterogeneity of what persistently precedes and exceeds such a singular and unilateral framing of time and space. In transforming abstract coordinates into worldly concerns they become both multiple and mutable. In the situated realisation of symbolic artefacts – the 'house', the 'square', the 'building', the 'street' – a complex historical provenance is secured in the shifting ecologies of an ultimately planetary landscape.

The interruption posed by the other and the elsewhere encourages the interrogation released in a oblique glance that cuts across the site and crumples the map with other times. Set free from the assumptions of disciplinary protocols secured in the institutional authority of architecture, civil engineering and public administration, the plan, the project, is here exposed to questions and queries that were previously silenced and unheard. The drive for transparency, and hence control, is deterritorialised and reterritorialised by what insists and resists the architectural and administrative will (to power).

All of this crosses and contaminates aesthetics with ethics. A closed, idealist and metaphysical imperative – the idea of 'beauty', the 'order' of reason, the 'rationality' of the plan – is transferred into the turbulent, open-ended grammar of a quotidian event. We are invited to look and think again; to touch and feel the experience of the everyday and the ordinary rendered extraordinary. In this transitory exposure (Heidegger's *aletheia* or revealing), a breach in the predictable tissues of a cultural and critical discourse is temporarily achieved. Here the solution proposed is neither permanent nor conclusive; it is precisely in 'solution', in the chemical and physical sense of the term: a fluid state in which diverse forces, languages and histories are suspended and culturally configured in the shifting currents of a worldly becoming.

Such an architecture, and aesthetics, shadows, occasionally spilling over, the borders of more permanent pretensions. As a border discourse it proposes tactical interruptions of a established strategy always seeking to realise its unilateral plan (often under the label of 'progress' and 'modernity'). It is in the borders, in a social and historical 'no man's' land where both civil rights, and frequently the very idea of the 'human', are suspended or yet to come, that it becomes necessary to elaborate another architecture of sense, another geometry of meaning: a poetics whose trajectory literally leaves the political present speechless.

This suggests that there is no one project, no single perspective, which is able to subordinate, discipline and edify space. The project, still dreaming of totalities and finitude, gives way to the critical passage that is always in elaboration. While the former is forever seeking home and the certitude of completing the plan, the journey, the latter is always under way beneath a sky too vast to possess. Here space, rather than passively received as an anonymous container, becomes a provocation. The space-time continuum is now cut up and redistributed in a disturbing semiosis: signs drift into other accounts, semantics are contaminated, deviated and subverted, ignored details and debris betray a history yet to be told. Space is re-articulated, transformed from a singular structure into a multilateral palimpsest that can be 'written' over, repeatedly. Freed from their supposedly objective status, space and temporality intersect into deviations from the unilateralism of 'progress'; both are redistributed in a narrative yet to be told.

As a traveling critical practice, a contingent architecture, traces of activity are disseminated in a manner that interpellate and interrogate the inherited. The prison house of habit, and its accompanying languages and conclusions, is transferred to a flotsam-ridden beach, the site of new departures.

In this critical exposure, tradition – historical, cultural and architectural – becomes the site of translation and transit. Here the tradition evoked is not the narrow history of Occidental architecture, but rather one that is articulated in the disturbing and interrogative tradition of dwelling on the earth beneath the sky. Here questions of freedom and action exist in proximity to the world rather than in debt to the abstract humanism of modern subjectivism (and its metaphysical culmination in the objectivism of technological rationalism). This suggests a precise move from architecture involved in the design of buildings to an architecture engaged in the care and construction of places. At this point, architects might be considered as meditators between the order, the discipline, they embody and the disorder or extra-disciplinary world they seek to house and accommodate.

Also at this point, the knowing and omnipotent eye of the architect (this was the preferred metaphor for God chosen by both Isaac Newton and William Blake), together with the very premises of Occidental humanism and its ocular hegemony, is suggestively replaced by the altogether more humble and immediate figure of the Disk Jockey. The DJ does not pretend to create from nothing, does not believe that language commences with his or her practice, but rather listens to, and takes in hand, existing languages seeking to extract from them a new rhythm, a diverse style, a more satisfying pulse and configuration. Beyond the geometry of space, exists an architecture, a manner of edifying and constructing places, composed in the rhythms, sounds, and everyday practices that exceed the plan, the project. This, for example, is the city that is cut up and mixed by the desires and needs of specific subjects.

Subjects in space speak through diverse histories and languages and, more directly, contest the auto-referential logic of abstract administration and architectural planning. In the space between buildings it is possible to hear a dialogue between place and identity. Here the dreamed symmetry of the project is continually subverted by the social, interrogated by the punctuation of the everyday. Here the object of the rationalist gaze, captured in the eye of the architect and the urban planner, becomes a subject; a subject who responds in a language that exceeds the logic of the project. Abstract bodies – citizens, people and individuals – become specific and differentiated realities. We pass from the geometric vision of space to its social dissemination and its historical articulation. We pass from mathematics to metamorphoses, from logic to language, from the grammar of the said to the on-going historical speech that constitutes and sustains us in the world.

So, how to plan, design and build in response to these shifting pressures and presences? How to reply to a history that is neither homogeneous nor amenable to a unilateral will? What that might mean involves a distinctive and explicit shift in the intellectual foundations and language of architecture itself. Architecture has historically tended to identify ground in the instance of edification. Before that moment space is considered literally meaningless, unconstructed and thereby unrepresentable. What if architecture were to build without the security of this *a priori* which protects it from what its reason cannot contain? At this point the abstract priority of geometry and design would be challenged by the historically and culturally invested ground upon which architecture both physically and metaphysically builds.

The awareness that architecture also embodies something that goes beyond its calculation, something that exceeds the more obvious techniques of projection, engineering and planning, leads to the insistence that architecture always occurs in a place, never an empty space. Architecture always builds on fractured, unstable ground. This is to intersect the art of rational construction – the will to construct an edifice: the metaphysics of building and the building of metaphysics – with the intercession, and protection, of the very question of our differentiated being in the world. There are forces within the languages of being, building and thinking that interrupt, break through and exceed the violent imposition of technical, 'scientific', 'rational' and unilateral solutions to that ancient and most present of demands: the unfolding question of how to dwell.

The contemporary critique and crisis of European

architecture paradoxically stems not from its failure and the threat of extinction, but precisely, as with so many other Occidental practices, from its ubiquity; from the fact that its grammar and reason has become universal. If architecture is about the narration and nurturing of tradition and place, of time and space, it can never simply assume an 'organic' relationship to what emerges from the immediate site. Every culture is historically the result of a hybrid and transit formation, borrowing and modifying styles and solutions that have been imposed, imported, borrowed, translated, bricolaged, adopted and adapted.

Considerations of architectural traditions necessarily evoke a return to a set of questions and resources that enable routing rather than rooting, connecting rather than collecting. This, in turn, leads to the valorisation of the inscriptive, and with it the lived-in quality of the terrain, the building, the habitat, over the prescriptive and the presumptions of the project, the plan. Here the building and the builder emerge in an unfolding cycle that is both material and critical, both historically and culturally specific. Such a sense of building involves working with the recycled, with the discarded and the re-signified; collaging, working over and working up the available in a further form, thereby overturning the hierarchical relationship between the rigidity of the monument and the fluidity of the trace and the ornament.

In a similar fashion, the classical sense of the city is consistently connected to the immediate history of a defined territory, the expression of an autochthonous culture. Nevertheless, in every city the roots invariably turn out to be routes, historical and cultural passages that traverse urban space offering entry into, and exit from, the immediate procedures of the metropolitan frame. So, the question becomes, how to think of both the city and the individual building as the crossroads between roots and routes; and, further, how to conceptualise the city constructed and constituted by mutable migratory flows and diversified cultural traffic. In other words, how do we think of the city no longer simply in terms of an apparently homogeneous historical-cultural texture, but as a permeable site suspended in the challenge of accommodating heterogeneity.

It is no longer merely a question of extending existing urban and civic space to offer hospitality to diverse, subaltern and hidden histories. It is rather we who are invited to reconsider and reconfigure our history in a reply to the interrogations that emerge in the streets of 'our' city, our 'home'. My own history, culture and sense of the world are rendered vulnerable by such histories: histories that are clearly impossible to capture in a unique point of view.

The historical and geographical name – Sao Paolo, Vienna, Lagos, London – of a specific urban space evokes multiple places that are sutured into a shared territory, producing the diverse configurations that cultural, historical and social bodies perform across its multiple planes. Within the on-going cultural and historical hybridisation of cities that we increasingly speak of today, the same urban space and time is re-signified, reworked and rewritten under the impact of diverse social perspectives, needs and desires. The same territory is rendered flexible and mutable as it continually migrates from one set of coordinates to another.

A location is always the site of cultural appropriation and historical transformation, the site of a particular manner and economy of building, dwelling and thinking. What emerges in the specific contours of each place is the subject who introduces agonism into the agora, confuting the regulated transparency of the plan with the unsuspected directions and opacities of the unplanned event. This is not simply a response that is restricted to a precise socio-cultural and historical site; for it simultaneously also represents a response to a wider series of questions that invest contemporary modernity. For what is proposed is an unfolding engagement with what falls off the planning table and is generally excluded from the project, what is in time and yet excluded from the temporalities of rationalism: a presence that threatens and challenges the authority of the planner. As Walter Benjamin has taught us, it is from an examination of what the city casts aside, its detritus and rubbish, that there emerge its innermost secrets and repressed logics.

In the modern rationalisations of urban space and development, such unrecognised places are for the moment literally nowhere. To disrupt the plan with its refuse, with its repressed matter, might therefore also be considered to underline a fundamental critical question: whether simply to synthesis and endorse an existing urban grammar, or to render it vulnerable to diverse horizons of sense that will modify, reconfigure and perhaps even lead to the abandonment of the language such a grammar proposes? In this vein, Occidental, or First World, architecture and planning would be connected to the more agile abodes that constitute housing, haven and recreation for the vast majority of the world's population who have neither the means nor daily stability to permit Occidental edifices.

Architecture as the site of critical work, is not only where buildings and cities are visualised, planned and projected, it is also where it becomes possible to listen to what the architectural practice and profession tends to silence or repress in its political economy of rationalising space. Can architecture respond to this other side, to those who do not fit into the abstract rigour of the plan, to those whose presence disturbs and contests its logics and rewrite the terms of accommodation according to another cultural design? Perhaps architecture might respond to such conditions, which are intrinsically among the structural conditions of what was once Western, but is now clearly a planetary, modernity, less by seeking to 'solve' such 'problems' and more by seeking to present them.

UNREALISED DEMOCRACY AND ART AFTER HUMANISM

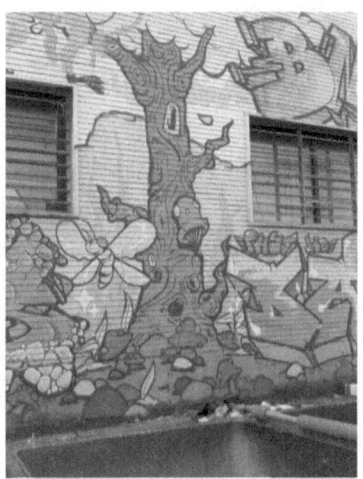

Naples 2011

The work of art allows us to glimpse, for an instance, the there in the here, the always in the now.

> OCTAVIO PAZ, 'PINTADO EN
> MÉXICO', EL PAIS, 7 NOVIEMBRE,
> 1983

HOW SHOULD CITIZENSHIP and its accompanying political and cultural agency be thought in the present-day context of transnational economies and international global imperatives? What has art got to do with it? Out beyond the pleas for solidarity, ecological responsibility and the recognition of a global multicultural heritage, the world is riven by local wars and planetary oppression and poverty. The brutal historical discrepancy between a rich, overdeveloped, minority and a poor, underprivileged and underrepresented, majority persists. I start from this cruel benchmark f or neither a profound structural redistribution nor ethical sea change able to challenge a narrowing horizon of expectation seems imminent. No one is giving up what they have.

Yet how then does one speak of citizenship, with its associated individual freedom for future action and freedom from immediate want, in a world where for the majority the concept crumbles into rhetorical dust before the implacable insistence of simply surviving? Or, rather, and this would be altogether more disquieting to consider: the demand for civic freedoms and justice from the fields and sweatshops of the rural and urban poor perhaps exceeds the classic sense of citizenship, peculiar to the property and propriety of urban modernity, that we are accustomed to employ?

The world, as the Palestinian intellectual Edward Said noted, is full of 'undocumented people', both in the bureaucratic and historical sense. (Edward Said, 'The Mind of Winter. Reflections on life in exile', *Harper's*. September

1984). This, he continued, is the non-cosmopolitan mass that exists beyond art, subjectivity and political and cultural representation. This is the reverse side, the dark side, of Benedict Anderson's noted insistence on the anonymous state of nationhood. Such peoples are 'exiled' in many ways; not only, and most obviously, as physical and material dislocation, but also economically, politically and culturally excluded from the agenda that dictates global development and 'progress'.

If the overdeveloped world requires the rest of the planet for economic and material resources, not to speak of the persistent presence of an abject alterity that cruelly mirrors and measures its own privileged identity, it also inadvertently manufactures a dramatic counter-space from where such an identity can be critically and dramatically reassessed. A state of powerlessness reveals potential powers.

Of course, nothing is encountered or lived in such stark black-and-white terms. Worldly configurations and locations are altogether more complex and hybrid in their formation and articulation. No one simply occupies a single category, destined to respect its premises forever. We live in a time simultaneously characterised by globalisation and crises, when it is necessary to return to the sobering structures in which political change and cultural transformation occur. Here it is important to recognise in the increasingly creolised conditions of metropolitan life not only the enrichment of the First World, but also the charged demands of other worlds that continue to exist far beyond the superficial grasp of a beneficial domestication.

Rendered vulnerable by proximity and the intersection of my world by the worlds of others, my identity is both contested and reconfigured in the reply to such 'intrusions'.

The countervailing excursion of other identities into 'my' world, induced by the breaking open and scattering of a previous locality, is invariably explained in terms of the radical configuration of late modernity. This is a historical moment that has been irreversibly invested by the interactive economical, social, cultural and political procedures of 'globalisation'. Yet my identity formation also invokes deeper historical currents. I am carried back at least to that instance in which the West and the 'world' are recognised and institutionalised as stable conceptual frames of reference in a particular period, place and population.

The instance the West identifies itself and simultaneously establishes the world in its image is clearly the historical moment when a certain intellectual and cultural formation confidently brings all under a single point of view, subject to a unique and unilateral perspective. Fears and desires are objectified, a sense of 'home' and 'abroad', of the domestic scene and 'otherness', firmly established. What today is experienced as a 'loss' is surely the taken-for-granted security of such premises. If this 'world picture' (Heidegger) is an integral part of the initial disposition of Occidental modernity, of its powers and the subsequent mapping of itself on the rest of the globe, then its contemporary interrogation, displacement, dislocation, perhaps alerts us to a potential epochal shift.

Notwithstanding the sociological understanding of symbolic interactionism and its notion of identity emerging in the relationship between self and society, here we meet an already more complex historical, cultural and psychic configuration. For at this point there emerges a historically elaborated self rather than a stable essence who is subsequently stitched or sutured into external political and cultural structures and processes. The 'out there'

LOCATION, BORDERS AND BEYOND   49

is also 'in here', the portal is porous, and whatever is repressed outlines the representation. This is to propose not merely a commonwealth of identification, but also an uncomfortable understanding of identity, including its deepest psychic recesses, being formed, articulated, extended and explored as a 'way in the world' (V.S.-Naipaul). This particular passage has precise historical, political and philosophical contours and configurations. Such is the space, and the limits, of modern, Occidental identity.

In the opening sequences of Werner Herzog's film *Cobra Verde* (1988), itself based on Bruce Chatwin's *The Viceroy of Ouidah*, there occurs a discussion between a Brazilian plantation owner and Francisco Manoel da Silva, the future slave trader portrayed by Klaus Klinski. It goes like this:

> I've another forty sugar plantations just like this one. I alone produce... 120.000 tons per year, and all of it goes to England. They've abolished the slave trade. They seize our ships, and yet without us they wouldn't have any sugar. Look at the way they buy the sugar, you'd think our rivers were overflowing with the stuff. It's grotesque.

In what the Caribbean poet Derek Walcott justly calls the 'bitter history' of sugar, here in the mid-nineteenth century we encounter an abolitionist Great Britain that since 1833 patrols the high seas, sequestering vessels involved in the slave trade, while continuing to enjoy the benefits of slave labour in the cotton that dresses its citizens and the sugar that goes into the tea on domestic breakfast tables.

This suggests that the much-quoted process of 'globalisation' is not simply a contemporary phenomenon, but is rather integral to the making of Occidental modernity from its beginning. Inaugurated with the possibility of reducing the world to a single map and a unique point of view, it represents the interests and desires of the Occidental observer. In this picture, the forced black diaspora out of Africa into New World slavery, the systematic exploitation and genocide of the Americas, emerge as central, not peripheral, to the global making of the modern Western world. Within this modernity the specific geopolitical location of the observer assumes a universal relevance: Occidental subjectivity and objectivity become one. This, of course, is humanism; or rather, if we want to hold on to the term, a restricted European humanism rather than the altogether more extensive worldly measure proposed by Aimé Césaire. With respect to its Occidental confines and practice, the latter is provocatively 'post-humanism'. All of which helps us to understand the political significance of humanism being re-inscribed in the history of locality and the limits of the point of view, the voice, the knowledge, that now finds itself speaking in the interstices of a heterogeneous, rather than homogeneous, world. This is a world, as Paul Gilroy consistently reminds us, that was historically constructed as much in terror as in reason.

It is impossible to free oneself from a past that has brought us to where and how we inhabit today. A citizenship, a democracy, historically formed in and through the structural inequalities that configured modernity is not an abstract moral category, but a historical process realised in regimes of power. Here, again, is the centrality proposed by

Eric Williams and C.L.R James, and recently reiterated by Paul Gilroy, of slavery to the making of Atlantic democracies. The expansion of commerce and civil rights are intertwined and directly inscribed in the stipulation of the American constitution by a slave-owning plantocracy. It is the extractive urgencies and exploitation of the New World that contextualises the political demands of the rising European bourgeoisie and the French Revolution, not to speak of its subsequent and paradoxical inspiration for the slave rebellion of its richest colony: Saint Dominique, later the first black republic of Haiti.

Such an altogether more undecided and heterogeneous understanding of modernity, composed of a series of always incomplete 'projects', serves to remind us of paths not taken, of possibilities blocked in blood and repression, of processes and procedures that even if they have disappeared recall the irreducible quality of the world and its multiple kind. No matter how powerful the appeal to the homogeneous prospect of 'progress', the 'archaic', the repressed and the unruly lace modernity, forcing the latter to register its transformation, its transit, its accidental quality and potential deviation. In this there lies a freedom, frequently unrealised, but waiting, in which we, too, are invited to participate.

To insist on the historically contingent is also to insist on the travel and elaboration of identity, subjectivity and 'citizenship' in languages where history encounters a reply that exceeds its institutionalised grammar. It is where the prosaic and the poetical exceed and interrogate inherited political identifications. It is where, to repeat Okwui Enwezor, 'we are moved to question whether the notion of democracy can be sustained only within the philosophical grounds of Western epistemology' (Okwui Enzewor, 'Democracy unrealised', *Platform 1_Documenta 11*, Kassel, 2001). Here the 'I' moves through the translated and translating space of the world becoming a subject for whom knowledge, sense and truth is irreducible to a unique point of view. Such a subject exists beneath, besides and beyond Occidental humanism. Opposed to the abstract, patriarchal universalism that humanism once proposed this is a subject that registers the diversification of centres and yet paradoxically is precisely more human in recognising its own specific limits and location. This sense of the self proposes a less assured and altogether more unguarded appropriation of where we come from (tradition, memory, heritage), as well of the historical, political and cultural structures and institutions in which we come to identify our passage through the world.

In the last two decades it has been, above all, the interruption of postcolonial studies that has sought to critically elaborate such a situation. Here there emerges the insistent reply of diverse worlds that are no longer separated, out there, at a distance, but which emerge in insistent border crossings that simultaneously register, resist and re-route the passage of trans-national modernity. From elsewhere arrive the 'them' who refuse to remain 'them', but who at the same time refuse simply to become 'us'; that is, who refuse to negate either the 'roots' or the 'routes' that renders a 'there' also a 'here'. The social, cultural and political import of this reconfiguration of 'here' and 'there' perennially echoes in the necessary and disquieting alterity of art: the aesthetics (and ethics) of disturbance that reveals a gap, an interval in the world, that signals a limit and establishes a transit, a passage elsewhere. It is in this space – historically nominated in such terms as the sublime, the uncanny, alterity – that the pedagogical languages of institutional identity, busily seeking to legitimate the narration of nation, citizenship and cultural subjectivity, are interceded and deviated by what refuses to make sense or speak in a prescribed way.

What this understanding of art holds out is the promise of interrupting such an order, of punctuating the homogenous, historical time of 'progress' that the West considers itself to represent. The art of the interruption, art as interruption, both brings to light our prescribed state – its limits and location in time and place – while also opening out on to the possibility of revisiting, reciting (in the sense of reworking) and re-siting (in the sense of transporting) those languages elsewhere. Here the prescribed is overtaken by the inscription, by the event, both artistic and ontological, that exceeds the grammar of expectancy and the semantics of institutional sense.

At this point, I would like to offer an example from popular metropolitan culture (although in this perspective the distinction between popular and élite cultures and art is increasingly of little significance) to underline how the space of the same city, of urban and youth culture, of music and the languages of identity, are translated and transformed to reveal other histories, cultures and identities within the same scene. In Gurinder Chadha's short film *I'm British But...* (1990), we see a band of south Asian musicians playing Bhangra music on a rooftop in Southall, London. Whether deliberate or not, this image recalls the scene of another group playing on a roof top in London some twenty years previously: the Beatles performing 'Get Back'.

In the repetition and doubling of the same metropolitan space and its associated grammar, there emerges the inhabitation of a shared languages – musical, metropolitan and of the media – to propose two different places. The former is that of Beatlemania, 'swinging London' and public white youth culture, the second is that of the diasporic music, culture and identity of Bhangra. What comes home in this proximity is not merely the articulation of cultural and historical difference taking up home in the same space, but that the later Bhangra formation is not so much something imported from the elsewhere of the Punjab, but is rather a local elaboration, springing out of the same complex historical and cultural locality as the earlier metropolitan Britain represented by the Beatles.

Art revisits and reworks the conceptual language that contains us. It is art, according to the 'post modern primitive', Cherokee artist Jimmie Durham, that is 'looking for connections that cannot, may be, should not, be made' (Jimmie Durham, *The East London Coelacanth*, Instiue of Contemporary arts video, 1993. In the insistence on the ontological event of language – as what occurs in the transitory configuration of sound, language, structure and vision: of our being in language and of our language in being – ideas about ourselves, about our democracy, our citizenship, our identity, are historically radicalised, transmuted into temporal processes. Here they are rendered vulnerable to the journey of interpretation, to the interruption of on-going, worldly interrogations.

This altogether more fractured perspective promotes the broken narratives of an elsewhere that refuse to fit into the unfolding of our lives. Any narrative, any accounting of the world, that is willing to receive and offer hospitality to the disturbance that uproots the *domus* and invites us not to feel at home when we are at home (as Adorno put it in *Minima Moralia*), renders the universal story many of us think we are living, more localized, limited, unsettled.

In the poetical power of languages to reconfigure space in a diverse understanding of place, location and identity, 'home' is rendered an altogether more open-ended and vulnerable habitat. The latter provides less the comfort and consolation of an eventual homecoming and more the perpetual point of departure for a journey destined to render uninhabitable previous understandings. This is why ideas of institutionalised multiculturalism and 'tolerance' are ethically insufficient and historical dead-ends. As the links between language, land and identity are inhabited by other histories and subsequently stretched to breaking point it becomes possible, and urgently necessary, to envisage a diverse worlding of the cultural, historical and political languages that represents us, and in which we represent ourselves.

Here it is, above all the West, so used to self-confirmation in every corner of the planet, which is localised. This brings us to Dipesh Chakrabarty's noted announcement of 'provincializing Europe.' More paradoxically, given that it is the habit of provincialism to consider itself always at the centre, it brings us to de-provincialise Europe. In breaching the borders of the local and the familiar to travel in a space produced by the transit of language itself, the ethical and the aesthetical are radically reconfigured. In the shift of language into a landscape no longer of exclusively occidental provenance, there is no single subject, history or culture is able to authorise the narration, the interpretation. There occurs a marked displacement from questions of property, origin and identity to more transitory differentiations in the heterogeneous making of the world. In this shift from the unilateral optics of representation (invariably concentrated in the subject-centred pragmatics of realism and the ideology that truth lies in transparency) to the altogether less guaranteed reception of poetic disturbance and interrogation, there emerges the potential of a cultural politics that exceeds both instrumental rationality and institutional arrest.

Borrowing from the observations and annotations that constitute Walter Benjamin's *The Arcades Project*, here there emerges the idea of collecting the refuse of the city, the fragments of the histories and languages of modernity that are found, as it were, casually in the streets, to create an unexpected critical mix. Once again, like a DJ revisiting and re-elaborating existing rhythms and riffs, this operation carries us towards other horizons of sense. Using the inherited languages and quotidian details in which we are enveloped to articulate a reply is to invest the prescribed with the inscribed, the pedagogical with the performative. In this manner, we are carried elsewhere into another, often unsuspected, configuration. In the 'scratch', in the montage of the 'mix', the borrowed, recycled and spontaneous but necessary practices of translation and bricolage provide a decisive critical metaphor for a more extensive understanding of contemporary cultural forms and forces. As Karen Hansen insists in her study of the second-hand West that dresses Zambia – *Salaula. The World of Secondhand Clothing and Zambia* (2002) – everything acquires a 'second life', a further meaning.

In this particular configuration, open to histories, memories and possibilities that arrive from elsewhere, identities cannot be lived in a state of understanding that is already fully established and realised. Identities become a point of departure, an opening on to the continual elaboration of becoming. This is to dispute a sense of modernity that as Friedrich Nietzsche noted in *Beyond Good and Evil*, attains the peak of nihilism in reducing the multiplicity of life to the metaphysical singularity represented by the presumed sovereignty of individual identity. The rationalist productivity of modernity, striving to harness and homogenise the world, is continually interrupted by its own languages transporting it elsewhere.

Unilateral desires and powers are deviated in a dissemination in which no single place can claim to own the language in which it appears and speaks. This is to insist on a limited sense of a world that is always susceptible to translation but cannot be transcended. The seemingly limitless reach of a unique and homogeneous understanding of technology and economy, of citizenship and political rights, of aesthetics and ethics, today the globe, comes to be arrested, brought up short, in the excess of language and time figured by art. From this unsuspected, often unwelcomed, supplement emerges the promise of the questions that continue to question.

ADRIFT AND EXPOSED: THE ART OF ISAAC JULIEN

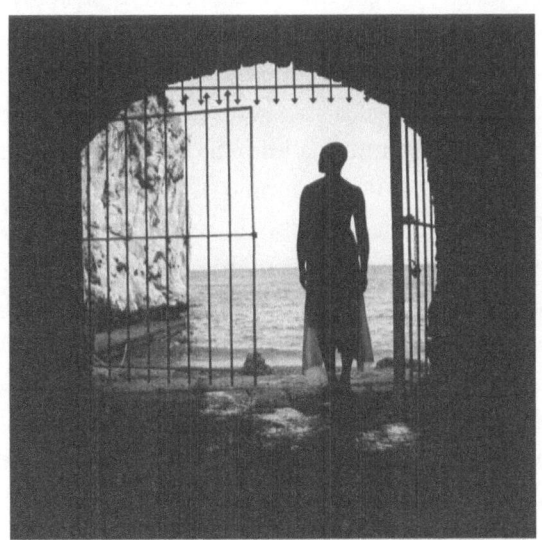

Western Union, Small Boats (2007)

NOT TO SEARCH for the reason of Isaac Julien's *Western Union: Small Boats* (2007), but rather to reason with the work, to speak in its vicinity: what follows is the log of one possible route. The trauma of modern-day migration, here most obviously deepened and dramatised by the dangers of crossing vast and inhospitable spaces – the Sahara and the Mediterranean Sea – is also the trauma of that split in the unified image of the world that seemingly reflects and respects only our concerns. Subsequent fragmentation disseminates the insistence of possible transits and impossible translations in which the refused, the expelled and the marginalised dissect and multiple the horizon. These are shards of history that are also parts of us. The narrative unwinds, confused by rhythms, tonalities and accents that befuddle the desire for a secure semantics and the reconfirmation of our world, of our possession of the account.

The images we confront are not mere representations, supports for a pre-existing narrative. They are themselves the narration, fragments of life lived, imagined, yet to come. The ubiquity of the sea in *Western Union: Small Boats* is not a mere background to a human drama, but perhaps that 'dumb blankness, full of meaning' (*Moby-Dick*) that speaks of an indifference to the liberal agenda in which 'ethical standing and civic inclusion are predicated upon rationality, autonomy and agency' (Cary Wolfe, 'Learning from Temple Grandin, or, Animal Studies, Disability Studies, and Who Comes After the Subject', *New Formations*, 64, 2008l, p. 110). The screen of the sea, like the cinema screen theorized by Gilles Deleuze, proposes the dehumanisation of images as the visual is freed from the subject and released to yield its autonomous powers. We are brought into the presence of a contingent, temporal relation, and the multiplicity of the present that is irreducible to its representation. This proposes the Deleuzian prospect of an altogether 'more radical Elsewhere, outside homogeneous space and time' (Gilles Deleuze, *Cinema 1: The Movement-Image*, University of Minnesota Press, Minneapolis, 1986, p.17). Between

LOCATION, BORDERS AND BEYOND   61

perception and a response emerges a zone of feeling, a resonance, a vibration, the power of an affect that inaugurates a passionate geography, an 'atlas of emotion' (Giuliana Bruno, *Atlas of Emotion*, Verso, London, 2007).

Presented with a time that exists beyond the linguistic act of nomination, we move beyond the subject that produces its image. This is why for Deleuze, and here we can return to the immediacy of Isaac Julien's work, art is not the expression of humanity, or an underlying unity, but is rather the release of the imagination from its human and functional home. Impossible we might say, and yet a necessary threshold that a non-representational and affective art seeks endlessly to cross. The veracity of the image is now to be located elsewhere, it is no longer a simple support – realism, mimesis – for narration, but is rather the narrating force. These are not images *of* life, but images *as* life; a life already imagined, activated and sustained in the image. There is not first the thought and then the image. The image itself is a modality of thinking. It does not represent, but rather proposes, thought. This is the potential dynamite that lives within the image: it both marks and explodes time. This is the unhomely insistence of the artwork, its critical cut and its interruptive force.

I met History once, but he ain't recognise me

DEREK WALCOTT, 'THE SCHOONER FLIGHT'

From the Black Atlantic to today's Mediterranean: a political and poetical passage in which the voice of the great

Creole poet of the Caribbean entwines with Walter Benjamin's philosophy of history while the past, no matter how much it is denied and ignored, continues to interrogate and illuminate the dangerous landscapes of the present.

If Ulysses purposefully crosses the Mediterranean, it is also a space that has also hosted those such as Polyphemus and Circe, Medea and Calypso, or Caliban, who have 'spoken of reasons that are inexpressible in the rationale of logos that triumphs in the Occident' (Monica Centanni, *Nemica a Ulisse*, Bollati e Boringhieri, Turin, 2007). In the tempest of the modern world, where a mythical Mediterranean is today brutally rendered in the fraught journeys of anonymous migrants, Caliban returns as an illegal immigrant, and Prospero's island, midway between Naples and Tunis in the sixteenth century drama, becomes modern day Lampedusa. For the language that frames the world always remains susceptible to appropriation by monsters, slaves, blacks, women, homosexuals, witches, migrants: the excluded who speak of unexpected, hidden, things that have not been authorised. Here the ghosts of history interlace the passage of poetics, creating powerful and disturbing images, difficult both to ignore and to digest.

In this disruptive geography it becomes both possible and necessary to rethink the limits of the world and the Mediterranean we have inherited; it becomes possible to open a vista on another Mediterranean, on another modernity. In this particular passage we are invited to follow a route indicated by Adorno in *Aesthetic Theory* where he suggests that art works 'provide the historical unconscious of their epoch'. Aesthetics declines into an ethics that promotes a poetics which exceeds the political thought that thinks itself capable of rendering the world transparent to its will. This anticipates a coming community.

Such a prospect is secured in the premise that the right to migrate is a human right that sustains a democratic sense of the world. Today's migratory movements – overwhelmingly from the impoverished souths of the planet – propose an unauthorised globalisation, a diverse worlding that has not sought our permission.

Faced with the political and cultural resistance to this prospect by the First World, it is the case to insist that the passages and perspectives traced by artistic languages propose an ethics-aesthetics capable of undoing, interrupting and interrogating the existing powers of explanation. This also means lodging such possibilities in the actual politics of panic where, under the apparent threat of illegal immigration, the liberal state has rendered the state of emergency permanent (to echo, again, Walter Benjamin). In the subsequent scenario it appears that we are the 'victims' and the immigrants the 'enemy' to resist. What the continual elaboration of legislative and repressive measures reveals is the persistent structural violence applied against the outsider, the foreigner.

Yet it is not the despised stranger who is the source of violence, rather the violence lies in our reception, in our refusal to receive the immigrant. Through processes of exclusion and definitions of subordination, the figure of the migrant turns out to be not external, but internal to the formation of modernity. In the elaboration of state legislation, in the social and political authorisation of government, in the legitimation of a consensual cultural lexicon, the foreign, immigrant, body, becomes central to the articulation of such key concepts as 'citizenship', 'culture', 'democracy' and 'freedom'. In such a matrix, repression, racism and the refusal of hospitality are not individual, but structural, qualities. They line and sustain the very idea of the modern nation state.

When one speaks of the social and cultural integration of the immigrant, of her eventual inclusion in the social and political sphere, it is automatically assumed that there already exists a clear and fixed definition of the culture that will eventually absorb (and annul) the foreign body. As Édouard Glissant would have put it, these are the certitudes that are cemented in intolerance. One's own culture is always certain, secure in its knowledge and authority; it is the other culture that must bend and contort itself to be recognised in its necessarily subaltern condition. Here there emerge a series of responses that insinuate themselves in multiple levels and sectors of contemporary society: from the law and state jurisdiction to that sense of identity elaborated in the texts of a national literature and history, to the diffusion of a 'common sense' sustained and amplified by the mass media. Everything seems clear, even obvious in its implacable clarity. However, the power of the language employed is, at the same time, the language of power.

If this brutal clarity serves to reinforce that sense of identity required by the modern nation state, it also reveals the refusal to interact with the interrogation posed by a seemingly foreign body. In the best of cases, there is the prospect of toleration rather than repression, and always the proposal of regulation through the application of *our* laws, and *our* economical, cultural and political needs. Here the integration and the assimilation of the stranger impose the public cancellation of all of his or her signs of historical and cultural belonging. Reduced to what the Italian philosopher Giorgio Agamben (after Hannah Arendt) has called 'bare life', the immigrant is required to strip herself of all those signs that might transmit a diversity that would disturb a culture that pretends to tolerate and eventually integrate her. The logic of superiority is explicit. It invariably endorses a racial supremacy.

Already stripped of all in the passage northwards, across the desert and over the sea, the migrant, if she or he makes it to the European shoreline, is required to become a 'bare life', denuded of his cultural costume, her social inheritance, reduced to a negated, private, memory. Yet the migrant does not arrive from an external and distant elsewhere, he or she is always and already a part of our world, part of a modernity that precisely reveals in the irruption of the migrant to be not only ours.

The ambivalence of our 'tolerance' towards other cultures is also the symptom of a complex, emerging modernity that refuses simply to reflect and respect only our needs. Those who arrive seeking work and a better life in the cities of the West have in a significant sense already arrived long before their departure from home in Africa, Asia or Latin America. They, too, are also modern subjects, subjected, as we all are, to the planetary political economy analysed by Marx 150 years ago. They, too, move in 'scapes' elaborated by capital, using the languages of a modernity that has become the modern world. In other worlds, this modernity is also theirs. They are not merely the 'objects' of planetary flows managed elsewhere, but are also 'subjects' able to bend, transform, translate and respond to the languages of modernity in senses, directions and possibilities not necessarily authorised by the old imperial centres and their modern revamping by global capital.

In *Western Union, Small Boats* (2007), we witness contorted black bodies gasping in the foam, abandoned on the beach in silver body bags amongst the sunbathers, or else writhing on the decadent palace floors of European hierarchies,. They replay history's obscurer rhythms, reaching into modernity's heart of darkness, collating the Black Atlantic, memories of slavery and racialized oppression to the present-day Mediterranean. Frantz Fanon, writing over 50 years ago, reminds us of this deadly objectification: 'I came into the world imbued with the will to find a meaning in things, my spirit filled with the desire to attain to the source of the world, and then I found that I was an object in the midst of other objects' (Frantz Fanon, *Black Skin, White Masks*, Pluto Press, London, 1986, p.109).

An immediate proximity is the side of 'globalisation', promoted by capital's radical deterritorialisation and reterritorialisation, which we are deeply reluctant to accept. We obviously prefer 'them' to be objectified as non-modern, tied to far-away places and traditions, anchored at a distance in their 'underdevelopment'. When we speak of tolerance, we are instinctively speaking of its one-sided exercise, or negation. We never refer to the toleration that might come from the non-Occidental world. Toleration and repression, the simultaneous extension and retraction of our world, take political and cultural forms that seek to halt the planet, circumscribe the disturbance and deflate the (global) processes in which immigration, together with structural poverty and ecological disaster, is one of the most dramatic announcements. A politics capable of receiving the historical and cultural complexity proposed by contemporary migration points to a rough, unwelcomed and unguaranteed passage between national, and even more local, pressures, and that 'thinking worldly' proposed many decades ago by the vital Mediterranean and Sardinian thinker Antonio Gramsci.

Yesterday's migrant who left Genoa or Glasgow bound for Buenos Aires, and today's migrant who leaves Senegal to be abandoned on Lampedusa, are separated in time and differentiated in space, but united in the same history. In the face of contemporary migration, there are frankly far too few willing to listen to those phantoms that constitute the historical chains that extend from Africa five hundred years ago to the coasts of southern Italy today and which link the hidden, but essential, narratives of migration in the making of modernity. To negate the memory evoked by the interrogative presence of the modern migrant is somehow to register an incapacity to consider one's own troubled and always-incomplete inheritance in the making of the present.

Amongst human rights, the right to migrate to better one's life should be recognised. After all, Europe's poor, from Scandinavia, Ireland and Scotland to the northern shores of the Mediterranean (including some 26 million Italians), have exercised this 'right' for several centuries. In this precise historical moment, however, we live in a world in which for the vast majority migration is a crime. Globalisation not only concerns the migration of capital at a planetary level, but also of bodies, cultures, histories and lives. While the former is considered inevitable, and often welcomed, the latter is both fervently resisted and increasingly criminalised. It has been estimated that in the coming decades one sixth of the world's population will be migrants, and many will almost certainly be criminalised for this.

Here the migrant's time – as a figure of negated and repressed time – becomes the migratory time of modernity. The distant shore and the marginal world that is hidden and ignored become immediate. It is literally figured and exposed by the body of the feared foreigner, the despised stranger and the abhorred migrant. The migrant's time creates a slash in our time through which modernity itself migrates and subsequently returns bearing other meanings. Here, in the time of the world, 'language will never be mine, and perhaps never was' (Jacques Derrida, *Monolingualism of the Other; or, The Prosthesis of Origin*, Stanford University Press, Stanford, 1998).

The images of *Western Union: Small Boats* propose an unavoidable encounter; its aesthetics expose an intractable ethics, a style of thinking. We are drawn to think within the images. The provoked interval remains open to interrogate that anxiety for normality which requires the expulsion of the migrant in order to continue to hegemonise the sense and direction of the world. It is perhaps only here, in the open and vulnerable scene promoted by art, that it becomes possible to promote for an instance an unexpected proximity: that moment of unhomeliness before the unexpected in which we temporarily recognise the other, the foreigner, as a part of ourselves. Such an interruption, affected by the autonomy of the image, proposes a diverse Mediterranean and modernity. As the great contemporary Arab poet Adonis suggests, it is probably only here that it is possible to inaugurate a dialogue between temporarily equal partners. Here in poetics, in the perpetual movement and migration of language, there already exists the critique of the actual state of affairs. Living language to the full is to touch the transit, the transformation and the translations of what is yet to come.

In this state of vulnerability, the discourses that secure and anchor us in the world, the authorised knowledge that has disciplined and directed our understandings – from historiography, anthropology and sociology to literature and philosophy – now find itself challenged by the same displacement and unhomeliness that it seeks to explain. To return to Derek Walcott, – 'I met History once, but he ain' recognize me' – perhaps it is only in the oblique gaze and the excessive and errant language of poetics that we manage to travel to where the rationalist analytics of the social and human sciences do not permit. For the artistic configuration of space-time, images as life and becoming, allow us to harvest the essential truth of the complex ambivalence of a historical constellation that does not simply mirror my passage, that does not simply mirror our passage...

It is the singular intensity of the images becoming *Western Union: Small Boats* that demands a new way of thinking.

PUSHING HISTORY OUT OF JOINT: ART AS ANACHRONISM

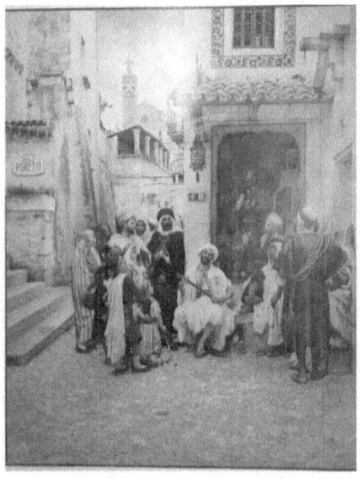

Gian Paolo Tomasi. Unoriente, Matera 2017

Whenever we are before the image, we are before time.

GEORGES DIDI-HUBERMAN, DEVANT LE TEMPS: HISTORY DE L'ARTE ET ANACHRONISME DES IMAGES

> The relevance of the essay is that of anachronism. The hour is more unfavorable to it than ever. It is being crushed between an organized science, on one side, in which everyone presumes to control everyone and everything else, and which excludes, with the sanctimonious praise of "intuitive" or "stimulating," anything that does not conform to the status quo... The essay... wants to blow open what cannot be absorbed by concepts, or what, through contradictions in which concepts entangle themselves, betrays the fact that the network of their objectivity is a purely subjective rigging.
>
> THEODOR ADORNO, 'THE ESSAY AS FORM"

It is precisely the anachronism that renders what we call history productive. Contrary to the presumed veracity of the documents and the facts seemingly guaranteeing a time scale that endorses a transparent chronology, the language of history, is always historically, culturally, politically and semantically placed. The 'facts' have to be dug up and elaborated, the 'documents' identified and interpreted. The explanation, the narrative, no matter how neutral or scientific it pretends to be, has to be constructed. Georges Didi-

LOCATION, BORDERS AND BEYOND 73

Huberman has consistently argued for the positivity of the anachronism as method in art history. I would suggest that the insistence of the anachronism also takes us further afield. Sanjay Seth has caught the epistemological stakes here in an instructively emphatic manner:

> ...historiography is an intellectual and cultural construct, one particular way of construing and constructing the past; at once a tradition of reasoning, a way of being, and a certain practice of subjectivity. The desire to write history is specific to certain people (societies, classes) and not others. It is connected to some phenomena – the emergence of the modern state, 'progress', scientific rationality – and not others, which it usually defines itself against (magic, gods).
>
> SANJAY SETH, 'WHICH PAST? WHOSE TRANSCENDENTAL PRESUPPOSITION?, POSTCOLONIAL STUDIES, VOL 11, NO 2, 2008, P. 215.

To express it bluntly, the European humanist elaboration of history, particularly when it is relocated and re-proposed within extra-European coordinates, itself becomes an implacable historical problematic. As Dipesh Chakrabarty put it, the plural claims of history inevitably lead to 'radically questioning the nature of historical time' (*Provincializing Europe: Postcolonial Thought and Historical Difference,* University of Princeton Press, Princeton,

2000, p 16). To introduce the different and multiple histories of sexuality, gender, ethnicity and race, is to register the violence of their subjection, silence and repression in order to permit a single authorisation of time. Not only, as Seth points out, does this challenge the anthropological premises of history orbiting around Man in the abstract and European subjectivity in real terms, but it exposes to 'external' coordinates and knowledge its universal presumptions.

To believe in the neutrality of language as providing a direct and unmediated access to the past is to ignore the very history of the medium being employed. It is what in a telling affirmation Jacques Derrida once called a form of 'linguistic imperialism' and 'colonial violence' (Jacques Derrida, 'Des Tours de Babel' in J F Graham, ed, *Difference in Translation*, Cornell University Press, London, 1985). Either the historian is an artist of the anachronism, redirecting and reworking the past into the present, or else is a ventriloquist who never quite gets his or her lines right. Reinhart Koselleck points to the critical recognition of this dilemma, arguing that the 'historian was confronted with the demand, both in terms of technique and epistemologically, that he offered not a past reality, but the fiction of its facticity' (Reinhart Koselleck, *Futures Past: On the Semantics of Historical Time*, Columbia University Press, New York, 2004, p. 206). And then the archive, however strictly or loosely defined, is always contemporary, a work in progress, an ongoing presence and practice that can never shut its doors on the past precisely because the present continues to charge the questions that ignites its authority.

Historians hate you to say this but the act of history as writing and research is an event in time and place. It, too, is a historical and performative practice. Understanding the past through the lens and language of another location in time and space is to understand that historiography is always of a time and place that is inevitably anachronistic with respect to its sources. This is provocatively to insist that to think of origins, both historical and cultural, is to think of contemporary configurations (Georges Didi-Huberman, 'The Supposition of the Aura: The Now, The Then, and Modernity' in Andrew Benjamin, ed, *Walter Benjamin and History*, Continuum, London, 2005). Remember how Walter Benjamin characterised origins as 'that which emerges from the process of becoming and disappearing' where there is no stable source but rather a 'whirlpool in the river of becoming' (Walter Benjamin, *The Origin of German Tragic Drama*, London, Verso, 2009, p. 45). This means that we are always working with a past that is inherently deconstructed with respect to any presumed totality or source. It is only by breaking apart the image of the presumed totality of the origin that it is possible to release fragments into the present telling of time. Historiography originates in this 'now'. Let us, mixing together the discussion on history and art, on the history of art and the art of history, consider this decisive statement by Georges Didi-Huberman:

> Before the image, however old it may be, the present never ceases to reshape, provided that the dispossession of the gaze has not entirely given way to the vain complacency of the "specialist". Before an image, however recent, however contemporary it may be, the past never ceases to reshape, since this image only becomes thinkable in a construction of memory, if not of the obsession. Before an image, finally, we have to humbly

> recognise this fact: that it will probably outlive us, that before it we are the fragile element, the transient element, and that before us it is the element of the future, the element of permanence. The image often has more memory and more future than the being who contemplates it.
>
> GEORGES DIDI-HUBERMAN, 'BEFORE THE IMAGE, BEFORE TIME', IN CLAIRE FARAGO AND ROBERT ZWIJNENBERG, EDS, COMPELLING VISUALITY: THE WORK OF ART IN AND OUT OF HISTORY, UNIVERSITY OF MINNEAPOLIS PRESS, MINNEAPOLIS, 2003, P. 33

All of this, despite the despair of those historians desperately seeking to tear away the veils of time and get back 'there', is not necessarily a loss or defect. Rather, it proposes a different orientation to time and meaning that disturbs the presumed 'plane of history' (Koselleck, op cit, p. 10). If we acknowledge that the past is a cultural and conceptual construction contaminated by the present and is continually being rewritten, reassembled and reassessed, then it becomes both possible and necessary to dismantle the confident European conceptual coinage of universal 'History' that replaced localised histories in the Eighteenth century and the positivism drawn from its subsequent Nineteenth century incubation as a discipline (Ibid, pp. 33–35). Appeals to the veracity of empirical evidence explained and guaranteed by the sovereignty of the Occidental male subject become although more critically complex and politically pertinent to the making of the postcolonial present. This is not only to challenge the metaphysics of empiricism and its illusions of an unmediated appropriation of the world, it is also to refute and decolonise an epistemology whose method is ultimately colonial in its presumptuous universalism.

Such an argument about history, or, rather its dominant modalities of reasoning and representation, poses an unsuspected rendezvous with a constellation of contemporary art practices. In their willingness to make connections and recover the past in a manner that would be unacceptable to the premises of the historical 'method', these practices frequently take us further into unsuspected critical configurations. To read time backwards, explicit in much contemporary art and a postcolonial take on the past, implicit, despited the declared neutrality of its methods, in historiography, renders both of our time and out of time with respect to purported origins and location.

As Khadija von Zinnenburg Carroll points out in a recent publication dedicated to the Aboriginal artist Julie Gough, this transforms the idea of 'anachronism' from a negative disparagement, deployed by historians to patrol and impose their disciplinary protocols, into a 'theoretical framework' with which to rethink the past, memory, history and artefacts (Khadija von Zinnenburg Carroll, 'Sartre's Boomerang: The Archive as a Choreographed Readymade', in Khadija von Zinnenburg Carroll, ed, *The Importance of Being Anachronistic: Contemporary Aboriginal Art and Museum Reparations*, Discipline/Third Text Publications, Kulin Nation/Wurundjeri, 2016, p. 21).

This is what Didi-Huberman calls the 'sovereignty of the anachronism' (Didi-Huberman, 'Before the Image', in Farago and Zwijnenberg, eds, *Compelling Visuality*, p 40).

It involves, as Foucault once put it, performing a cut that inaugurates a new field of enquiry and study (Michel Foucault, 'Nietzsche, Genealogy, History', in P Rabinow, ed, *The Foucault Reader*, Pantheon, New York, 1984). Clearly I am not intending to suggest that this perspective has not been encountered and debated among historians. Reinhart Koselleck spent much of his professional career as a historian wrestling with the linguistic and social mediation of concepts in seeking to break apart the presumed unicity of 'historical time' and better understand how 'in a concrete situation, experiences come to terms with the past' (Koselleck, *Futures Past*, op cit, p. 3). The critical subtlety and sensitivity of Koselleck, however, is an exception. Historians of all hues largely tend to avoid the epistemological and deeper political consequences of the question as they continue to write and research the past as documented objectivity.

Decolonising modern historiography, its methods and premises, involves the recognition of this (historical) problematic. To act against the normative interpretation of time and adopt a 'strategic anachronism' means to implode the present with what an existing order has repressed and annihilated to ensure its claims on the past. To work the present in order to better understand the past, that is to reason anachronistically, is precisely to construct archives that permit the retrieval of other histories, of the histories of others. The histories of the subaltern, of slavery, of forced diasporas, of feminism, gender and sexual rights, is surely about this necessary disturbance; that brushing of history against the grain proposed by Walter Benjamin which produces another history. This means to insist on the disruptive quality of a history that until that moment was unauthorised and invisible (Walter Benjamin, 'Theses on the Philosophy of History', in *Illuminations and Reflections*, Schoken Books, New York, 1969).

To intervene in the recording and registration of the past is not simply to decolonise a certain narrative hegemony, it is also to query perspectives and procedures, the paradigm and the premises, that produced a particular object-document and a type of history as opposed to another. Such an amplification and extension of 'history' as a mode or reasoning and explanation clearly carries us beyond the disciplinary purvey of historians. Here the recent work of artists and critics, often themselves coming from the margins of subaltern and invisible histories, provide us with an altogether more extensive and dynamic theoretical script.

Sharp distinctions between the factual and the fictional evaporate in a critical narrative willing to award the imagination in delivering to the present a more complex sense of the past (Zinnenburg Carroll, *The Importance of Being Anachronistic*, op cit, p. 27). Giving form to what has apparently disappeared returns a loss that lives on in the present. Necessarily incomplete and ambiguous it produces another context, both analytically and politically. Documenting and bringing to our attention such practices and procedures – whether directly, obliquely, ironically or bitterly – the archive is traversed and trespassed so as to be de-linked from a unique authority (History, the museum, the nation-state) in order to promote a new series of negotiations. Historical temporality comes unstuck from a single measure secured in the 'homogeneous time'(Benjamin) of the presumed 'progress' of the West and its version of the world. This is where, for example, the anachronism of archeology can lead to the critical honesty of what Yannis Hamilakis calls 'assemblage thinking' which:

> involves by implication the commingling and the contingent co-presence of diverse temporal moments; this is a multiplicity of times, of various pasts and various presents, but also a multiplicity of temporal modalities: geological times, archaeological/historical times, human experiential times, non-human animal experiential times.
>
> YANNIS HAMILAKIS, 'SENSORIAL ASSEMBLAGES: AFFECT, MEMORY AND TEMPORALITY IN ASSEMBLAGE THINKING', CAMBRIDGE ARCHEOLOGICAL JOURNAL, VOL 27, NO 1, P. 173.

Here to insist on the anachronistic as a method, and consider the 'historical determination of time' (Reinhart Koselleck), is to evidence the juxtapositions and entanglements that wrench the colonial past 'from the terms in which they were once cast' (Zinnenburg Carroll, *The Importance of Being Anachronistic*, op cit , p. 44). This is deliberately to unsettle an established consensus in which the conditions of semantic, cultural and... political production are consigned to their 'origins' in a separate past; now they need constantly to re-negotiate their place in the world as ongoing presence. As the artist Julie Gough puts it, referring to the (t)here of the 'impossible return' to the place of her Aboriginal ancestors, this is 'to amplify the unattainable resolution' (Julie Gough, 'The Possessed Past Museums: Infiltration and Outreach and The Lost World (Part 2)', in Zinnenburg Carroll, ed, *The Importance of Being Anachro-*

nistic, op cit, p. 66). It is to weave out of the mounting debris of the past another relational web drawn from what is apparently out of time and out of place. It is to hold on to the discontinuous in the productive montage that makes up the present, over and against the 'temporal logic of historicism that posits a strict division between past and present' (Ellen Smith, 'Obsolence and Ephemera in Postcolonial History: the Work of Julie Gough', in Zinnenburg Carroll, ed, *The Importance of Being Anachronistic*, op cit, p. 138). It to insist on a 'history beyond the historical record' (Ibid, p. 146).

Let us return to the conversation between contemporary postcolonial art and the institution of history as a form of memory and knowledge. Both operate with the idea of the archive. If the postcolonial archive is one that comes from the future – its histories have been silenced and repressed and are still to be registered and narrated – the historian, on the contrary, presumes his or her objectivity is guaranteed by the absolute passage of time and the sharp separation of the past from the present. If this teleological chronology apparently guarantees a historical 'method', we also instinctively know, simply by looking around and moving through the world, that what we call history has neither ceased nor been cut off from our present. The past has not passed.

This unresolved tension, which I would suggest presents us with an instance of critical freedom, is probably most fruitfully put to work in contemporary postcolonial art. The names and works that can be evoked at this point are many. So many that perhaps we should refer to a 'postcolonial turn' in modern art; that is, that revaluation of the archive and the associated documenting of historical time and place that operates a cut and proposes a critical discontinuity not simply within modern art practices, curating and art history, but across the knowledge formation we call modernity. Through a sensorial and corporeal engagement, the works of Mona Hatoum and Lorna Simpson, or Isaac Julien and John Akomfrah, Tracey Moffat and Jimmie Durham, propose a configuration of signs and senses in which the ethical and the aesthetic, the past and the present, become inseparable. They register the repressed return, reworking and releasing what conventional history is rarely able to acknowledge.

Let us take Isaac Julien's multi-screen film installation *Ten Thousand Waves* (2010). Commencing from the helicopter footage of the tragedy of anonymous Chinese labourers, illegal immigrants, drowning in Morecambe Bay in 2004 while cockle picking, we are simultaneously drawn through the sensorium of the nine screens into multiple scenarios that take us to the Shanghai film industry of the 1930s, to the goddesses and myths located in a place now called China, through Jah Wobble's musical score (remember post-punk PIL?) to the poetry, calligraphy and *mise-en-scene* of the installation itself. The mixture of location and temporalities sustained in the plurality permitted by contemporary audio-visual technology produces a complex constellation. We are pulled in diverse directions. We encounter a splintering of time whose fragments morph into the audio-visual immediacy of the present. The images are beautiful, the narratives intriguing, but there is also something more occurring here.

Ten Thousand Waves is not only good to look at and experience, it is also good to think with and practice. For beyond the immediate terms proposed by trans-locality, globalisation and the unpacking of modernity through registering the ghosts of its anonymous victims, the work raises questions that touch on how we understand, receive and reason the present: reason, not rationalise. In that Nietzschean derived distinction lies the rub. For what a postcolonial art work like *Ten Thousand Waves* produces and sustains is certainly neither a definitive conceptual order nor a conclusive arrangement of meaning. This is to emphasise temporal and spatial multiplicity as essential to the violent and ambiguous making of modernity; both to its political economy and to its art.

Here the processes of producing time and space, history and geography, as unfinished historical business comes to the fore. This is clearly neither a neutral experience nor merely an aesthetic act. Drawing on the languages and lexicons of the established art canon is central precisely to the degree that they are revisited, cut up and reworked so that other times and places emerge. The chronology of the West, and its associated teleology of 'progress', is necessarily interrupted, broken up and reassembled. Other maps emerge, other coordinates come into view. This cuts both aesthetically and critically into our understanding of the formation of the present.

Here we have moved from considering the art work as a restricted object of art history and aesthetics, to registering it as a critical apparatus or disposition. Both aspects live on and survive within it. Yet in inviting us to look and think again there emerges the supplement that burdens the circulation of art with the anachronism: the present drawn into and reconfigured by a negated past that we can never fully recover nor know. Here, despite the crushing consensus imposed by capital, postcolonial art deliberately works the gap and sustains the contradictions that render its language critical. If, while pushing up against the white walls of the modern museum and art gallery, postcolonial art does not escape capture in the institutional frame it nevertheless disturbs its premises. It has led to some of the most significant critical debates within contemporary culture, practising the political and historical reach of art while reworking the very terms and languages of the present. Precisely through refusing to be in harmony with the exiting state of affairs, inciting a past still to come, imposing the anachronism, such art and criticism constantly propels us into another history.

ACKNOWLEDGMENTS

'The Stones in Language' was first published in *Southerly* (vol.66, n.2, 2006), while 'Whose modernity? Whose Home?' appeared in *The New Centennial Review* (volume 3, n.2, Summer 2003). 'Troubled Ground' was prepared as an essay for the catalogue *urbanism – for sale* accompanying the exhibition of feld72 at the Sao Paolo Architectural Biennale in 2007. 'Unrealised democracy and art after humanism' was prepared for the Vienna platform of *Documenta 11* in 2002, and 'Adrift and exposed' for the catalogue accompanying Isaac Julien's *Western Union: Small Boats* installation at the Centre for Contemporary Art in Warsaw in 2009. 'Pushing History out of joint: art as anachronism' was published in the on-line edition of *Third Text* in 2018.

 I would like to thank the editors of these respective publications for initially providing me with the space to express the perspectives that are now brought together in this publication.

 I thank Kathleen Petyarre and Gallerie Australis for permission to reproduce Kathleen Petyarre's work.

 Apart from the images from Isaac Julien's *Western*

Union, Small Boats, by kind permission of the author, the other images are mine, including that of the cover taken at Orhan Pamuk's *Museum of Innocence* in Istanbul.

Finally, I would like to thank Johan Höglund as Director of Linnaeus University Centre for Concurrences in Colonial and Postcolonial Studies for providing me with the space, support and calm to write 'Pushing History out of joint: art as anachronism'.

ABOUT THE AUTHOR

Iain Chambers lives and works in Naples, Italy. He is the author of several books, including *Migrancy, Culture, Identity* (1994), *Mediterranean Crossings. The Politics of an Interrupted Modernity* (2008) and *Postcolonial Interruptions, Unauthorised Modernities* (2017). He presently teaches at the University of Naples, «Orientale».

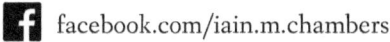 facebook.com/iain.m.chambers

www.ingramcontent.com/pod-product-compliance
Lightning Source LLC
Chambersburg PA
CBHW020452220526
45464CB00002B/962